John

The Gospel of Light and Life

John

The Gospel of Light and Life

John: The Gospel of Light and Life
978-1-7910-2148-1
978-1-501-80534-9 *eBook*

John: Large Print Edition
978-1-501-80535-6

John: Leader Guide
978-1-501-80536-3
978-1-501-80537-0 *eBook*

John: DVD
978-1-501-80541-7

John: Youth Study Book
978-1-501-80548-6
978-1-5018-0549-3 *eBook*

John: Children's Leader Guide
978-1-501-80550-9

For more information, visit www.AdamHamilton.org.

Also by Adam Hamilton

24 Hours That Changed the World

Christianity and World Religions

Christianity's Family Tree

Confronting the Controversies

Creed

Enough

Faithful

Final Words from the Cross

Forgiveness

Half Truths

John

Leading Beyond the Walls

Love to Stay

Making Sense of the Bible

Moses

Not a Silent Night

Revival

Seeing Gray in a World of Black and White

Selling Swimsuits in the Arctic

Simon Peter

Speaking Well

The Call

The Journey

The Walk

The Way

Unafraid

Unleashing the Word

When Christians Get It Wrong

Words of Life

Why?

ADAM HAMILTON

Author of *The Way, The Journey,* and *24 Hours That Changed the World*

JOHN

The Gospel of Light and Life

Abingdon Press / Nashville

John
The Gospel of Light and Life

ISBN 978-1-7910-2148-1

The Library of Congress has cataloged the hardcover edition as follows:

Names: Hamilton, Adam, 1964- editor.
Title: John : the gospel of light and life / Adam Hamilton, author of The way, The journey, and 24 hours that changed the world.
Description: Nashville, Tennessee : Abingdon Press, 2015. | Includes bibliographical references.
Identifiers: LCCN 2015039226 | ISBN 9781501805332 (binding: hardback)
Subjects: LCSH: Bible. John--Criticism, interpretation, etc.
Classification: LCC BS2615.52 .H35 2015 | DDC 226.5/06--dc23 LC record available at http://lccn.loc.gov/2015039226

21 22 23 24 25 26 27 28 29 30—10 9 8 7 6 5 4 3 2 1
MANUFACTURED IN THE UNITED STATES OF AMERICA

To Professor Jouette M. Bassler,
whose course on the Greek exegesis of John
helped me to see that there's more to the
Gospel of John than meets the eye.

Contents

INTRODUCTION

John is unique among the Gospels.

We call Matthew, Mark, and Luke the Synoptic Gospels. *Synoptic* is a Greek word that means "to see together," and it is appropriate here because these three Gospels are very similar. They share much of the same material and general outline of Jesus' life.

John's portrayal of Jesus is markedly different from that of the Synoptics. Many of the events recorded in John are not found in the Synoptic Gospels. John's Gospel is largely set in and around Jerusalem, whereas the Synoptic Gospels record Jesus' ministry in the Galilee. Jesus *sounds* different in the Synoptic Gospels, where he speaks in parables and in a straightforward, plainspoken way. But in John, Jesus speaks in metaphors that are more obscure.

In the Synoptic Gospels, Jesus describes the kingdom of God and the ethical imperatives demanded in the Kingdom. (The Kingdom is mentioned seventy-five times in Matthew, Mark, and Luke.) In John's Gospel, the focus is not on the kingdom of God (only mentioned twice), but on Jesus himself as the one who reveals God. The author of John presents Jesus as the *source* of life, and he wants to be sure we "get" this.

In Matthew, Mark, and Luke, Jesus calls people to follow him. In John, Jesus calls people to believe in him and to abide in him. Both following *and* believing in Jesus are important dimensions of Christian discipleship. Clearly, we need the insights and invitation of both John and the Synoptics.

To understand and appreciate the Gospel of John, it's helpful to have a little background. First, the Gospel is officially anonymous. As in the other Gospels, the author is not identified by name. John 21:20-25 does mention a "disciple whom Jesus loved." However, the phrasing could mean that the author was drawing upon the written and oral testimony of the beloved disciple or that the beloved disciple himself was the author. Modern scholars debate this. The weight of church tradition identifies the beloved disciple as John, the brother of James, and further that this John was the author of the Gospel that bears his name. In this book, we'll assume that John was the author, but we want to acknowledge that the scholarly debate exists.

Most scholars date the Gospel of John to some time during the last two decades of the first century. By this time, according to tradition, all the other disciples had been put to death. Only John remained, the last living witness among the first apostles. John would have known that Gospels and pre-Gospels written by others were circulating, but his would be different from theirs. His would include material theirs did not have. And his would focus more intentionally on the question of Jesus' identity and importance. If the author was, in fact, John the disciple, he had spent a lifetime reflecting upon the significance of Jesus.

None of the Gospels are, strictly speaking, biographies of Jesus. But John's Gospel, more than any of the others, is something of a spiritual or theological commentary on Jesus' life, death, and resurrection. We're not meant to read it as a journalist's or biographer's account of Jesus' life. In John, details of events and even the words of Jesus are not so much about what actually happened, though clearly they are rooted in what actually happened. Instead they are about the *meaning*—the spiritual significance—of Jesus' life. For this reason, I believe, Clement of Alexandria (A.D. 150–215) described John as "the spiritual Gospel."

As John explores the questions of the identity and meaning of Jesus, I invite you to do the same. This book is structured to help you explore the major themes of John. It is meant to be read alongside the Gospel. With that in mind, we have included the entire text of John. At the end of each chapter you'll find a portion of the Gospel, and if you read each portion after you read the chapter, by the end of the book you will have completed the Gospel of John.

As you read John, I encourage you to approach the text actively, thrusting yourself into its pages and pondering how its words speak to the meaning of Jesus for your life. To help you do that, I encourage you to answer three questions with each passage that you read:

- What is said in this passage about Jesus?
- In this passage, how does Jesus bring life to me?
- What response do these verses require of me?

This book is meant to offer pointers and keys to reading John. It is not a verse-by-verse commentary, but instead a guide to John's major themes, exploring their meaning and offering clues that will help you read all of John. The book is six chapters long, a good length for use in a small group study. A DVD is also available, with 10-15minute segments meant to help small groups explore John's Gospel.

In John 20:31 we read, "These things are written so that you will believe that Jesus is the Christ, God's Son, and that believing, you will have life in his name." My hope is that this little volume will help you to believe and find life in Christ's name.

Chapter One

The Word Made Flesh

In the beginning was the Word and the Word was with God and the Word was God. The Word was with God in the beginning. Everything came into being through the Word, and without the Word nothing came into being.
(John 1:1-3a)

1

The Word Made Flesh

Let's begin our study of the Gospel of John with what is called the Prologue, one of the loftiest and most inspiring passages in the New Testament. It lays out the major premise of the Gospel, so it's a good way to start our exploration.

In spite of its weight and importance, the Prologue is actually quite short, consisting of just the first eighteen verses of John. However, because of their weight and importance, we could easily write an entire book just on these verses.

Most scholars believe that portions of these first eighteen verses were an early Christian hymn influenced by Greek and Jewish philosophical ideas. John incorporated the hymn, reworking it a bit, because it captured profound ideas about who Jesus is and the meaning of his life.

Before delving into the meat of this section, I want to point out what you no doubt have already noticed, that the Gospel begins with these three words: "In the beginning." You'll recall that another book of the Bible starts with these same words. Genesis 1:1 starts, "In the beginning. . . ." John's use of these words is no accident. He is pointing back to the creation story. For now, I merely want you to notice the reference, and I'll say more about it at various points throughout the book.

The premise of the entire Gospel, so beautifully introduced in the Prologue, is that Jesus embodies God's Word. The Greek term used by John for Word is *Logos*. It is the root of our words *logic* and *logical* and is seen as the suffix of words such as *biology, psychology,* and *zoology*. It can simply mean "word," but in the Greek world it often meant much more. It conveyed knowledge, wisdom, reason, and revelation. The Stoics, a group of philosophers in the third century B.C., spoke of *Logos* as the mind and purpose of God that permeated all of creation. In the first verse of John's Gospel, he speaks of a Word that was in the beginning. This was the mind and heart of God. The Word was "with God" and "was God." John goes on to say: "Everything came into being through the Word, and without the Word nothing came into being" (John 1:3a).

Remember that in Genesis, God *spoke* and creation happened: "God said, 'Let there be light!' And so light appeared. God saw how good the light was" (Genesis 1:3-4a). In God's speech—the Word—were the heart, character, will, and creative mind of God. It was the logic that created the cosmos. I think of the physicists and cosmologists who speak of the universe in terms of principles and mathematical equations or the biologists who unravel human DNA. John affirms that it was God's logic, God's Word, that set the universe in motion.

It was by this logic that we "live, move, and exist" (Acts 17:28). The Word is God's heart, God's reasoning, God's mind, God's purposes, God's character, God's creative power, and God's desire to reveal himself to us.

Up to this point in the Prologue, no first-century philosopher or theologian would object to what John has said. Jews and Greeks would agree that the universe is logical and that its logic is the mind of God. God is logical. Further, God desires to speak to us. The premise of the Bible is that the God who created the universe wants to be known by human beings. Again, few in the first century would have debated this lofty and powerful statement.

But then we come to verse 14, where John makes this outlandish claim: "The Word became flesh and made his home among us. We have seen his glory, glory like that of a father's only son, full of grace and truth." In other words, as John begins his Gospel on the life of Jesus, he is telling us that God's heart, mind, reason, logic, will, and desire to reveal himself to the human race have been wrapped in human flesh and have come to us as a person, Jesus Christ! The very mind that ordered and brought forth creation took on flesh and "spoke" to humanity in Jesus Christ.

John ends the Prologue by restating his outlandish claim in different words: "No one has ever seen God. God the only Son, who is at the Father's side, has made God known" (1:18). We speak of this idea of the Word becoming flesh as the Incarnation. The Latin word *Incarno* means "to enflesh."

"No one has ever seen God. God the only Son, who is at the Father's side, has made God known." (John 1:18)

John does not tell us how this happened, how Jesus embodied God's word. In fact, the church would spend the next three hundred years working out how to express Jesus' simultaneous divinity and humanity, and the nature of the Trinity. John, however, is not concerned with those complexities. He is concerned that you and

I know that Jesus embodies the Word of God. The Word of God comes to us most completely, most clearly, and most compellingly, not in a book, but in a person. Thus, everything John will say about Jesus points to who God is and what God is like. When we pray to God, we picture Jesus Christ. We come to know who God is by looking at Jesus. We abide in God by abiding in Jesus. The invisible God is made visible in Jesus Christ.

For many generations before Jesus was born, people believed in God. Prophets and lawgivers and preachers tried to describe God based upon their experiences of God and their own logic. But then in Jesus, God stepped into our world. His birth, life, teachings, miracles, death, and resurrection answered the questions "Who is God?" and " What does God expect of us?"

This earthshaking idea, expressed so beautifully and uniquely in John, is why Jesus is so central to our faith as Christians.

LIGHT SHINING IN THE DARKNESS

What came into being through the Word was life, and the life was the light for all people. The light shines in the darkness, and the darkness doesn't extinguish the light. (John 1:3b-5)

Permeating John's Gospel are two ideas: light and life. Light is a metaphor for several things and is always understood over and against darkness. Sometimes darkness is synonymous with spiritual blindness or a failure to understand what it means to be human. Sometimes darkness refers to evil.

Jesus came to dispel the darkness. He came to be the light for us. At our Christmas Eve services at Church of the Resurrection, we turn off all the lights and stand in the darkness. Babies cry and people cough and little children squirm, and it's uncomfortable for a while. In the darkness we talk about the darkness we experience at times in our lives. Then we bring in one candle from the back of the room. This candle represents Jesus. We read the Prologue of John and remember that Jesus came to bring light to our darkness. He dispels the darkness. You're likely familiar with the service: each person has a candle, and we pass the candlelight throughout the room, saying to one another, "The light of Christ." Soon the entire room is filled with light. John would be pleased, for it captures a premise of his Gospel: Christ came to push back the darkness in our world and in our lives.

We can't appreciate the light until we recognize the darkness. We see darkness in the news when we read about another act of violence in a school, a movie theater, a community square. We see it in the natural disasters that leave communities in chaos. We see it in the terrorist attacks and the heinous crimes committed against humanity, sometimes in the name of God. For some, the darkness comes when our spouse leaves or we lose our job or we receive a frightening diagnosis. And, of course, all of us walk through the valley of darkness when someone we love dies. These are all expressions of the darkness into which Jesus offers light, comfort, healing, and hope.

In John, darkness is a metaphor not only for evil, despair, and hopelessness, but for losing our way. Those who walk in darkness are lost and blinded by sin. Jesus is the light that can guide us, helping us see the way by the things he taught and by what he showed us in the example of his life. He showed us forgiveness and love and grace. He showed us compassion and kindness and mercy. He not only removes our sin, he shines a light on the path we're to take. Jesus embodies the words of the psalmist: "Your word is a lamp before my feet and a light for my journey" (Psalm 119:105).

I'm reminded of times when I've taken cave tours, and I was so grateful for the guides who held flashlights and helped us navigate through the darkness. We are followers of Jesus as he illuminates the way we're meant to follow. You know the way: loving God and neighbor, forgiving others, loving enemies, speaking truth, showing compassion.

In his Prologue, John reminds us that human beings at times love the darkness rather than light. But he also makes clear that the darkness could not overcome Christ's light. When we walk in the light of Christ, when we listen to, hear, and accept God's Word, we have life.

Jesus came to be the light for us so that we, as his followers, might in turn be light for others. As those who have the light of Christ and walk in the light of Christ, our task is to dispel the darkness—to bear the light of Christ and embody his light.

IN HIM WAS LIFE

In John's Prologue, notice what the light leads to: life. Jesus, the Word made flesh, offers life. This is a hugely important idea in John, who tells us that he wrote his Gospel "so that you will believe that Jesus is the Christ, God's Son, and that believing, you will have life in his name" (John 20:31).

John uses the word *life* forty-seven times in his Gospel. Most of the time it is Jesus who speaks of the life he offers, and usually he describes it as "eternal life." The most famous of John's statements about life is what Martin Luther called the "gospel in miniature," John 3:16: "God so loved the world that he gave his only Son, so that everyone who believes in him won't perish but will have eternal life."

For John, eternal life is not just what happens after we die, though it certainly includes life after death. For John, eternal life begins *now.* It is a state in which we are not afraid of death, in which we experience a new life in Christ. Jesus himself puts it this way: "I assure you that whoever hears my word and believes in the one who sent me has eternal life and won't come under judgment but has passed from death into life" (John 5:24).

Jesus dramatically illustrates the promise of eternal life by raising Lazarus from the dead in John 11. He demonstrates it most powerfully in his own resurrection. But he also teaches us about living in God's kingdom here and now. As we know Jesus, trust him, abide in him, listen to his voice, and follow him, we experience forgiveness, hope, love, and a purpose-filled existence. We become a part of a community, a family, where we find love. We walk in his light and carry his presence to sustain us and keep us.

We are awakened from spiritual blindness and death as we trust in Jesus—in his words, his life, his death, and resurrection. We live differently because we know that death is not the end. Death is just a period at the end of a sentence before a new sentence begins. It's just the end of one chapter—we might even say the prologue—and the beginning of the great adventure God has in store for us.

Death is just a period at the end of a sentence before a new sentence begins... and the beginning of the great adventure God has in store for us.

How do we achieve that life? In John, the primary way is by believing in Christ and learning to trust in him. We trust that he speaks the words of life. We trust that he is the way, the truth, and the life. And in trusting him, we begin to walk with him.

Russell D. Moore expressed it well in an article he wrote for *Christianity Today*:

> For too long, we've called unbelievers to 'invite Jesus into your life.' Jesus doesn't want to be in your life. Your life's a wreck. Jesus calls you into his life. And his life isn't boring or purposeless or static. It's wild and exhilarating and unpredictable.[1]

That's what is meant when we talk about having a personal relationship with Jesus Christ. It is trusting in him, walking with him, talking with him, listening for him, believing him, following him, knowing him. In Jesus we find life, "and the life was the light for all people" (John 1:4).

In Jesus' Arms

When our children were small we would tuck them into bed at night, tell them a story, remind them of God's love, and then pray with them before they went to sleep. To this day I kneel before bed and entrust to God's care my now-grown children and my granddaughter, imagining Jesus holding them in his arms.

Several years ago Dick Bandy, the father of my wife, LaVon, passed away. He lived a great life and was a very special person in our lives. He lived outside Decatur, Illinois, but came to Kansas City often. The last time was just a few weeks before he died. At bedtime each night, LaVon walked him to his room. She tucked her father into bed and told him that she loved him, then we would kneel at his bedside and entrust his life, and our lives, to God. These were beautiful and tender moments, and ones in which we drew strength from our trust in the Good Shepherd, Jesus, whom Dick had sought to follow much of his life.

Dick returned home, and as he faced his final hours we prayed with him one last time by phone, then drove all night to be with him at the hospital. He died just minutes before we arrived. In that moment of darkness he walked toward the light of Christ and trusted in that light.

I anointed his head with oil in the hospital room shortly after he died. Then we gathered around and prayed. Tears flowed as we said good-bye. But we knew this: Dick belonged to Jesus Christ, the same Jesus who came to reveal God to us, the same Jesus who shines light on our moments of darkness, the same Jesus who offers us life and who said, "I am the resurrection and the life. Whoever believes in me will live, even though they die" (John 11:25). Dick belonged to Jesus, and we placed him in Jesus' arms. And now we find strength to live with hope, because we know that our lives, too, belong to Christ, and someday we will see Dick once more.

John writes that we might have life in Christ's name. I'd like to invite you to trust in Christ—to decide that you not only will follow him in the way that Matthew, Mark, and Luke followed, but that you will trust in him who offers light and life to all who believe.

Jesus, I trust in you, that you are God's Word in the flesh. I trust that you are the light of the world. Illuminate my darkness. Help me to walk in your light and to love and follow you all of my days. In your holy name. Amen.

The Gospel of John: Part One

John 1 (CEB)

Having considered the meaning of John's Prologue, I invite you to read the entire first chapter of John.

JOHN

Story of the Word

1 In the beginning was the Word
and the Word was with God
and the Word was God.
2 The Word was with God in the beginning.
3 Everything came into being through the Word,
and without the Word
nothing came into being.
What came into being
4 through the Word was life,[a]
and the life was the light for all people.
5 The light shines in the darkness,
and the darkness doesn't extinguish the light.
6 A man named John was sent from God. 7 He came as a witness to testify concerning the light, so that through him everyone would believe
in the light. 8 He himself wasn't the light, but his mission was to testify
concerning the light.
9 The true light that shines on all people
was coming into the world.
10 The light was in the world,
and the world came into being through the light,
but the world didn't recognize the light.
11 The light came to his own people,
and his own people didn't welcome him.
12 But those who did welcome him,
those who believed in his name,
he authorized to become God's children,
13 born not from blood
nor from human desire or passion,
but born from God.
14 The Word became flesh
and made his home among us.
We have seen his glory,
glory like that of a father's only son,
full of grace and truth.
15 John testified about him, crying out, "This is the one of whom I

[a]Or *Everything came into being through the Word,/and without the Word / nothing came into being that came into being. In the Word was life*

said, 'He who comes after me is greater than me because he existed before me.'"

16 From his fullness we have all received grace upon grace;
17 as the Law was given through Moses,
so grace and truth came into being through Jesus Christ.
18 No one has ever seen God.
God the only Son,
who is at the Father's side,
has made God known.

John's witness

19 This is John's testimony when the Jewish leaders in Jerusalem sent priests and Levites to ask him, "Who are you?"

20 John confessed (he didn't deny but confessed), "I'm not the Christ."

21 They asked him, "Then who are you? Are you Elijah?"

John said, "I'm not."

"Are you the prophet?"

John answered, "No."

22 They asked, "Who are you? We need to give an answer to those who sent us. What do you say about yourself?"

23 John replied,

"*I am a voice crying out in the wilderness,*
Make the Lord's path straight,[b]
just as the prophet Isaiah said."

24 Those sent by the Pharisees 25 asked, "Why do you baptize if you aren't the Christ, nor Elijah, nor the prophet?"

26 John answered, "I baptize with water. Someone greater stands among you, whom you don't recognize. 27 He comes after me, but I'm not worthy to untie his sandal straps." 28 This encounter took place across the Jordan in Bethany where John was baptizing.

29 The next day John saw Jesus coming toward him and said, "Look! The Lamb of God who takes away the sin of the world! 30 This is the one about whom I said, 'He who comes after me is really greater than me because he existed before me.' 31 Even I didn't recognize him, but I came baptizing with water so that he might be made known to Israel." 32 John testified, "I saw the Spirit coming down from heaven like a dove, and it rested on him. 33 Even I didn't recognize him, but the one who sent me to baptize with water said to me, 'The one on whom you see the Spirit coming down and resting is the one who baptizes with the Holy Spirit.' 34 I have seen and testified that this one is God's Son."

[b] Isa 40:3

John 1:35

Jesus calls disciples

35 The next day John was standing again with two of his disciples.
36 When he saw Jesus walking along he said, "Look! The Lamb of God!"
37 The two disciples heard what he said, and they followed Jesus.

38 When Jesus turned and saw them following, he asked, "What are you
looking for?"

They said, "Rabbi (which is translated *Teacher*), where are you staying?"

39 He replied, "Come and see." So they went and saw where he was
staying, and they remained with him that day. It was about four o'clock
in the afternoon.

40 One of the two disciples who heard what John said and followed
Jesus was Andrew, the brother of Simon Peter. 41 He first found his own
brother Simon and said to him, "We have found the Messiah" (which is
translated *Christ*[c]). 42 He led him to Jesus.

Jesus looked at him and said, "You are Simon, son of John. You will
be called Cephas" (which is translated *Peter*).

43 The next day Jesus wanted to go into Galilee, and he found Philip.
Jesus said to him, "Follow me." 44 Philip was from Bethsaida, the hometown of Andrew and Peter.

45 Philip found Nathanael and said to him, "We have found the one
Moses wrote about in the Law and the Prophets: Jesus, Joseph's son,
from Nazareth."

46 Nathanael responded, "Can anything from Nazareth be good?"

Philip said, "Come and see."

47 Jesus saw Nathanael coming toward him and said about him, "Here
is a genuine Israelite in whom there is no deceit."

48 Nathanael asked him, "How do you know me?"

Jesus answered, "Before Philip called you, I saw you under the fig tree."

49 Nathanael replied, "Rabbi, you are God's Son. You are the king of
Israel."

50 Jesus answered, "Do you believe because I told you that I saw you
under the fig tree? You will see greater things than these! 51 I assure you
that you will see heaven open and God's angels going up to heaven and
down to earth on the Human One."[d]

Chapter Two

The Miraculous Signs of Jesus

On the third day there was a wedding in Cana of Galilee. Jesus' mother was there, and Jesus and his disciples were also invited to the celebration. When the wine ran out, Jesus' mother said to him "They don't have any wine." Jesus replied, "Woman, what does that have to do with me? My time hasn't come yet." His mother told the servants, "Do whatever he tells you." (John 2:1-5)

As Jesus walked along, he saw a man who was blind from birth. Jesus' disciples asked, "Rabbi, who sinned so that he was born blind, this man or his parents?" Jesus answered, "Neither he nor his parents. This happened so that God's mighty works might be displayed in him." (John 9:1-3)

2

The Miraculous Signs of Jesus

The Gospel of John contains some of the most beautiful and lofty passages in the Gospels, as well as some of the most confusing. John's Gospel begs to be read at a deeper level, at times even read allegorically; there is almost always more to a story than meets the eye. Many of the details have meaning beyond simple description, so we must pay close attention as we read them.

John's stories are not meant merely to tell you what Jesus did and said; they are intended to convey the deeper meaning of Jesus' life. As we noted in the introduction, they don't provide a journalist's perspective; they offer a theological perspective on Jesus.

When I consider the way John portrays Jesus, I think of the Dutch painter Vincent van Gogh and his postimpressionist style.

John's portrayal of Jesus is a bit more postimpressionist than representational.

With that in mind, let's take a minute to consider Van Gogh and one of his most famous paintings. Van Gogh had a deep love of God. He felt called to be a pastor, served briefly in England as an assistant to a Methodist pastor, and sought to enter seminary. Unable to pass the entrance exam, he went on to serve as a volunteer missionary, but he seemed to rub people the wrong way. (You may know that Van Gogh struggled with mental illness.) As a result of his actions, the church told him he couldn't serve anymore. From that time on, not surprisingly, while he continued to have a deep faith he felt only antipathy for the church.

Some think both his love for God and his struggle with the church are captured in his remarkable painting, *The Starry Night.** You've probably seen it. The painting shows a town and a church at night, and above them is the most amazing sky: the moon and stars whirl like pinwheels overhead. Many see the lights in the sky as representing Christ, the light of the world, or the light of God's love. Some houses in the village have this light in them as well, perhaps signifying the light of Christ in the hearts and lives of people. But there is no light at all in the church, which is in the very center of the painting. This may be Van Gogh's way of venting his frustration with the church of his day—a cold building without the light of Christ in it.

I've looked at this painting my whole life, and only recently did I begin to see its possible message about the light of Christ. How did I miss that? It was because I wasn't looking for it. I wasn't paying attention.

When you read a story in John, part of what makes it interesting (and even fun) is asking: is there more to the story than meets the

* This painting is currently part of the collection of The Museum of Modern Art, New York, New York. You can see it at http://www.moma.org/collection/works/79802.

eye? Does this or that detail mean something? There are always at least two levels at which these stories can be read: the straightforward level, in which water is changed into wine or the eyes of a blind man are opened, and a deeper level, which answers questions such as those I posed earlier: Who is this man Jesus? How does he affect my life? What is required of me?

John's descriptions of Jesus' miracles provide good examples of these multiple levels. John calls the miracles "miraculous signs." A sign points toward something else. Scholars often refer to John 2 through 12 as the "Book of Signs." These chapters contain seven of the signs—miracles that point to the identity of Jesus and the nature of life in Christ. Some believe the fact that John records seven of these signs is likely significant, since in ancient times the number seven was seen as representing wholeness or completeness.

Let's turn our attention to two of the miraculous signs described in John—the first sign and the sixth sign—and how we might study them to find deeper meaning.

CHANGING WATER INTO WINE

The first miraculous sign is found in John 2:1-12. Jesus and his disciples had been invited to a wedding, and a wedding banquet followed. Jewish wedding banquets in the first century are thought to have lasted seven days. These occasions were then, as weddings and wedding receptions are today, among the great moments in the life of a family and one of the most joyful times in any community. It's for this reason that the Bible often associates heaven with a wedding banquet.

But remember, there is a deeper meaning to John's stories. This story is not only about Jesus providing wine for a wedding but also about the life he offers to each of us. Twice in his parables, Jesus uses a wedding banquet as a sign of the messianic time to come. Even at the end of the Book of Revelation, we see Jesus preparing the "wedding banquet of the Lamb" (Revelation 19:9).

At the wedding banquet described in John 2, the wine ran out. This was terribly embarrassing for the host. Remember, at that time water was not always safe to drink, and people often drank wine at every meal. Wine offerings were made to God as a sign of life and joy and goodness. And though some passages of Scripture warn about drunkenness, there also are many that portray wine as a good part of life. (There are over 250 references to wine in the Bible, and most are positive.)

In the story, Jesus' mother came to Jesus and told him the wine had run out. Then she told the servants to do whatever Jesus told them. We don't know that Mary was expecting a miracle at this point, only that Jesus was going to make sure the wine problem was solved. I think she may have imagined Jesus going with them to the local wineseller to purchase more wine. With this in mind, she gave instructions to the servants at the wedding banquet.

But remember, John's stories of Jesus are intended to have a deeper meaning. Here's a question that might help you see the deeper meaning here: Who are Christ's servants today? The answer: we're his servants.

Now, listen again to verse five: "His mother told the servants, 'Do whatever he tells you.'" Note that when the servants did as they were told, a miracle occurred—water was changed to wine; the ordinary was converted to the extraordinary. John may have been saying, similarly, that if all of us do as Christ tells us, then our ordinary lives can become extraordinary.

You might say, "Is that really what John meant?" We can't be sure, but so much of John's writing has multiple levels that the little clues and phrases may well point to this deeper meaning.

Using the same approach, let's consider some other details about this miraculous sign.

> Nearby were six stone water jars used for the Jewish cleansing ritual, each able to hold about twenty or thirty gallons. (John 2:6)

Why does John tell us the jars were used for Jewish rites of purification? He could have said simply, "There were six stone jars." And why does he tell us they were stone jars, when typically they would have been clay? It seems likely to me that this detail takes us back to the Old Testament, where, in Ezekiel God says, "I will remove your stony heart from your body and replace it with a living one" (Ezekiel 36:26). John's story is not just about Jesus changing water into wine, but it is instead about how life in Christ is richer and more joyful than the ritualistic religion of first-century Judaism.

> Jesus said to the servants, "Fill the jars with water," and they filled them to the brim. Then he told them, "Now draw some from them and take it to the headwaiter," and they did. The headwaiter tasted the water that had become wine. He didn't know where it came from, though the servants who had drawn the water knew. The headwaiter called the groom and said, "Everyone serves the good wine first. They bring out the second-rate wine only when the guests are drinking freely. You kept the good wine until now."
> (John 2:7-10)

The servants didn't just fill the jars; they filled them "to the brim." I think John is telling us that Jesus wants to fill us up completely. We're meant to be overflowing, as a cup "runneth over." Remember, the overarching theme of this Gospel is that we might have life in Christ's name.

Notice that the wine Jesus created from the water was not just any wine, but the really *good* wine. And not just a little, but a lot: perhaps 150 gallons! The wine that Jesus created was better than the wine the guests had been drinking before.

In the Hebrew Bible, wine is often used as a metaphor or a sign of blessings and goodness and joy. Here it represents the life Jesus offers, a life of joy, peace, hope. When you choose to come to Christ, you find a life filled with those qualities. It's better than the life you had before. When Jesus took water and turned it into wine, he showed us that he can take what is ordinary and make it extraordinary. In this story, John is showing the rich, full life offered by Jesus, as contrasted with the sometimes empty religious rituals of first-century Judaism.

When Jesus took water and turned it into wine, he showed us that he can take what is ordinary and make it extraordinary.

John does not include the traditional Last Supper narrative in which Jesus takes bread and wine and asks his disciples to "do this in remembrance of me" (Luke 22:19). However, in John 2 when Jesus speaks of wine, and in John 6 when Jesus speaks of bread, many believe John is unpacking the meaning of Holy Communion.

In the Synoptics, the wine at the Eucharist represents Jesus' death, his blood shed for us. But John may intend the wine at the Eucharist, viewed through the lens of this story, to represent the source of joy and life that we find in Christ. This feeling is expressed well in one of my favorite Communion hymns: "I come with joy to meet my Lord, forgiven, loved and free. . . ."[1]

Again, you might wonder if John really meant for us to interpret the stories so metaphorically and symbolically. I'm aware that at first this type of interpretation may seem tenuous, but I think you'll find that the more you read John, the more it appears that the stories and the details point to this kind of deeper meaning, something that scholars who have made John their life's work are quick to point out.

I've suggested that this first story connects the joy and mirth of wine at a wedding banquet with the Eucharist. There's a similar connection with the pagan religions of the Greco-Roman world. Keep in mind that John wrote both for Christians living in the Greco-Roman world and for those who were not yet Christians but who had an interest in Jesus Christ. These readers were well acquainted with the pagan deities, one of whom was Dionysus or Bacchus, the god of wine and mirth. (You may be familiar with the word *bacchanal*, which refers to a party where one may become intoxicated or to a person who is a drunken reveler.) In ancient times, Dionysus or Bacchus promised a life of joy, mirth, and happiness. However other attributes were anger, rage, and drunkenness. His story was well known by both Jews and Gentiles of the first century.

There was a story told about Bacchus by some of his priests that he himself had changed water into wine. Thus, when John tells his story of the wedding banquet, he is showing that Jesus was able to do what the mythical Bacchus could do. More to the point, John is demonstrating that the life offered by Jesus is richer and more joyful, not only than the ritualistic Judaism of his day, but also than the paganism of Bacchus. (Remember that the wine Jesus provided at the wedding banquet was found to be better than the wine offered by the groom, which was the kind of ordinary wine associated with Bacchus.)

Most of us are not in danger of pursuing a faith of empty religious ritual, but we *are* likely to be tempted by Bacchus—to make sensual pleasure our god. There's nothing wrong with sensual pleasure. Sexuality is a good gift from God. Wine, consumed in moderation, is considered in Scripture to be a blessing. But when we make Bacchus our god, we become slaves to something that doesn't ultimately give life but takes it away. Taken to extremes, Bacchus will change us for the worse, whether he leads us to alcoholism or materialism or sexual addiction. Jesus, on the other hand, offers us, in the words of Paul, "what is truly life"(1 Timothy 6:19). So, like the servants in the story, we're meant to "do whatever he tells you," and when we do, Jesus will transform the ordinary life we live into something extraordinary.

OPENING THE EYES OF THE BLIND AND REVEALING TRUE BLINDNESS

Let's take a look at another of the seven miraculous signs. (I'll then encourage you to explore the remaining five on your own.) The sixth miraculous sign, the healing of a blind man, is so important in John's Gospel that it fills the entirety of chapter 9. Since John covers the entire earthly ministry of Jesus up to the Last Supper in just twelve chapters, devoting one chapter to this miraculous sign indicates that its message is very important. (You might even want to turn to John 9 in your Bible as you read the rest of this chapter.)

As described in John, one day Jesus and his disciples were in Jerusalem and saw a blind beggar. The disciples asked, "Rabbi, who sinned so that he was born blind, this man or his parents?" (v. 2).

This question tells us how some Jews thought in the first century and how some Jews and Christians still think today: If something bad happens to you, it must be punishment for something you have done wrong. This is a major assumption in much of the Old Testament—that adversity is a punishment for sin. (The Book of Job, a magnificent epic of Hebrew poetry, counters this view that was so prevalent in mainstream Jewish theology.) Many of us fall into this way of thinking when something terrible happens. We are desperate to understand why it happened and believe that our suffering, or someone else's, must be the result of sin.

But Jesus replied to the disciples, "Neither he nor his parents. This happened so that God's mighty works might be displayed in him" (v. 3).

I love this. Jesus is clear that this man's blindness is not a punishment from God but instead is an opportunity for God's work to be revealed. Of course, sometimes when bad things happen it is a consequence of our own actions. But we should be very cautious in attributing our suffering to God, or in believing that suffering is God's punishment. The Gospel teaches that Jesus bore the burden of human sin on the cross. He was, in the words of John, "the lamb of God who takes away the sin of the world!" (1:29).

Jesus is clear that this man's blindness is not a punishment from God but instead is an opportunity for God's work to be revealed.

I can't read this passage in John without thinking of Jay Williams. Jay and Cathy were longtime members of our church who had been trying for years to have a child. Finally they gave birth to a little girl they named Taylor, and just a few months later Jay was diagnosed with a rare and aggressive form of cancer. I went to see Jay immediately after his diagnosis. As we sat in his living room, I told Jay that God does not give us cancer. His cancer was not given to punish him or to teach him. Just as you would not inject cancer cells into your children to teach them or punish them, neither does God give us cancer. The nature of human cells is that sometimes they mutate in harmful ways, and while these mutated cells are typically destroyed by the body, sometimes they begin to multiply rapidly. Jay said he believed that too.

Jay went on to say that he'd just been reading the story about the blind man in John 9. He added, "Jesus said this happened so that 'God's works might be revealed' (v. 3 NRSV). That's what I'm praying for. I'd like to be healed. The doctors say it isn't likely with this form of cancer. I'm praying for healing, but even if it does not happen, I'm praying that God will use me and this cancer to reveal and accomplish his works."

In the end Jay died, but not before he touched the hearts of hundreds of people at his workplace, in his neighborhood, and at our church. God does not send suffering our way, but God can use it and work through it. As we invite God to use our suffering, and to bring good from it, our suffering takes on meaning. We find strength to bear it and sometimes even joy in the midst of it.

In the days before he died, while in the ICU and often in pain, my wife's father, Dick Bandy, was thanking each of the doctors and nurses who were caring for him. He was finding ways to make them laugh. They'd come in and ask, "How are you feeling, Mr. Bandy?" and he would reply, "Mostly with my fingers!" They had to think about it for a moment, and then they'd laugh. It's been said that people are like stained glass windows, that their true beauty is revealed when the darkness comes and a light shines brightly within and through them.

William Barclay reminds us that it is not only our own suffering that allows us to display God's works; we can also display God's works when we offer love and compassion to others who suffer. Barclay writes, "To help a fellow man in need is to manifest the glory of God, for it is to show what God is like."[2]

This is very much like what Jesus says in Matthew: "In the same way, let your light shine before people, so they can see the good things you do and praise your Father who is in heaven" (5:16). So, our daily mission is to look for opportunities to reveal the work of God, to be living signs pointing to the love of God.

Let's go back to our story about the blind man. After making it clear that the man's blindness was not a punishment, Jesus stopped, took saliva, mixed it with dirt to make mud, and placed it on the blind man's eyes. Then he instructed the man, "Go to the pool of Siloam and wash" (v. 11). It was a strange request. Jesus could easily have healed him on the spot. Why make mud and send the man to wash?

There are several ways to make sense of this story. One way points back to the creation story in Genesis. John has already given a nod to the creation story in the opening words of the Gospel, "In the beginning. . . ." You'll recall that in the story of Adam and Eve, God took the dust of the earth and from it formed the first human being (Genesis 2:7). Here in John 9, Jesus, who is the Word of God enfleshed, takes dust, mixes it with spittle, and heals a blind man. In this "miraculous sign," Jesus is shown to be the one who heals what is broken in God's world and in ways that mirror what God did at creation in the Old Testament.

In Genesis, God asked the man and woman not to eat the fruit of a certain tree; in John 9, Jesus asked the man to go wash in the pool. In Genesis, brokenness and pain came into the world when the first humans disobeyed God and ate of the fruit; in John 9, brokenness and pain were healed when the man obeyed Jesus and went to the pool to wash. The miracle would not have happened if the man had not trusted Jesus and done as he had said, just as the water would not have been turned into wine if the servants had not done as Jesus had commanded them at the wedding banquet.

It's interesting to note that in both miracles, water played an important role. Water is important in John. He mentions it twenty-nine times, more than Matthew, Mark, and Luke combined. It is likely that several of these references hint at the significance of baptism. Certainly in the story of the blind man, we're meant to think of baptism when Jesus asks the man to wash in the pool of Siloam.

I believe one reason John devotes so much time to this particular story is because the blind man represents each of us. We are all born blind beggars. According to John, you are walking in the darkness until you've seen the light, until you've allowed Christ to enter your life, until you've trusted him and begun to follow him. It doesn't mean that before that time you are a terrible person; it just means you haven't yet seen the light. Our eyes are opened when we hear his voice, trust his words, and do as he commands. When the blind man decides to trust Christ, obey him, and wash in the pool, suddenly the man can see, paralleling our Christian journey involving trust, obedience, and baptism.

The final thing to notice in this story is that after the man was healed, a great fuss was made about it. The blind man who could now see created quite a stir. It seems that Jesus healed him on the Sabbath, and Jewish law forbade healing the sick on the Sabbath unless the person's life was in danger. This man had been blind since birth and his life was not in danger, so the man was brought before the religious leaders who demanded an explanation. When the man told them Jesus had healed him, they said Jesus was a sinner. One of my favorite lines in the story is verse 25, in which the man answered, "I don't know whether he's a sinner. Here's what I do know: I was blind and now I see." Don't you love that? It's meant to be the testimony of every Christian: I once was blind but now I see.

This sixth miraculous sign ends by offering a powerful contrast between the blind beggar who listened to Jesus' voice, trusted him, obeyed his commands, washed, and thus came to see; and the religious leaders who refused to listen to Jesus and condemned him as a sinner. The question John intends the reader to ask is: who in this story is really blind? It's not the blind man, but the religious leaders, the very ones who believe they can see.

In describing the man's story, this miraculous sign, John asks us, in effect, "Are you blind, or can you see?" When we trust in Christ, seek to do his will, and are washed in the waters of baptism, we find our eyes opened. (Interestingly, reading about Paul's conversion in Acts, we find that Paul was blinded just before his conversion, and it was not until he was baptized that his sight was restored.)

When we trust in Christ, seek to do his will, and are washed in the waters of baptism, we find our eyes opened.

Both the healing of the blind man and the changing of water into wine ultimately point to the same message: Christ offers life. This life is richer and more meaningful than the ritualistic Judaism of his day or the sensuality offered by Bacchus. Christ is the light of the world. As you trust him and do as he asks, your eyes are opened to see life as it is and to see God as he is.

This leads me to the familiar story of John Newton, a sailor working in the slave trade in the mid-1700s. Newton had been upbraided by his captain for being even more profane than the other sailors with regard to his language, his drinking, and his character. But he began reading books on the life of Christ, and after a storm at sea killed nearly the entire crew of his ship, he chose to put his trust in Christ. Over the years he laid aside the personal flaws his captain had pointed out, and finally he laid aside the slave trade altogether. Eventually he became a pastor. Then, as he pondered the plight of the slaves, he joined William Wilberforce in seeking an end to the slave trade in the British Empire. He wrote a pamphlet that was sent to every member of Parliament and was reproduced in the tens of thousands. Newton lived long enough to see the official end of the British Empire's slave trade in 1807.

In 1779 he wrote a poem, a prayer that he invited his congregation to recite with him at the end of his sermon one Sunday. The words were meant to describe the change that comes when we trust in Christ and obey his words. They were later set to music.

> Amazing grace! How sweet the sound
>   that saved a wretch like me!
> I once was lost, but now am found;
>   was blind, but now I see.[3]

As John Newton discovered, it is when we trust in Christ, believe in him, and do what he asks of us that the chains fall off, that we become found, that we are delivered, that our eyes are opened, and that we find life in his name.

I offer three specific invitations as you ponder these miraculous signs in John:

- For those who have not said yes to Jesus Christ, I invite you to do that today.
- If you are suffering, invite God to use your suffering for good purposes—to bring meaning to it by displaying God's work through it.

- When you see someone else suffering, help carry the load or alleviate the suffering, that through you the glory of God might be revealed.

Lord, I want the joy and life that you offer, to drink of the best wine as I put my trust in you and receive Holy Communion. Help me to choose your way over the ways of "Bacchus." May my suffering and adversity be an opportunity for your works and glory to be revealed. Please use me to alleviate the suffering of others. And I pray for you to open my eyes that I might truly see. In your holy name. Amen.

The Gospel of John: Part Two

John 2–5 (CEB)

John chapters 2–5 includes two of the "miraculous signs" of Jesus, as well as other stories that capture some of the prominent themes we've been discussing. Grayed text is from the previous chapter.

John 1:35

Jesus calls disciples

35The next day John was standing again with two of his disciples. 36When he saw Jesus walking along he said, "Look! The Lamb of God!" 37The two disciples heard what he said, and they followed Jesus.

38When Jesus turned and saw them following, he asked, "What are you looking for?"

They said, "Rabbi (which is translated *Teacher*), where are you staying?"

39He replied, "Come and see." So they went and saw where he was staying, and they remained with him that day. It was about four o'clock in the afternoon.

40One of the two disciples who heard what John said and followed Jesus was Andrew, the brother of Simon Peter. 41He first found his own brother Simon and said to him, "We have found the Messiah" (which is translated *Christ*[c]). 42He led him to Jesus.

Jesus looked at him and said, "You are Simon, son of John. You will be called Cephas" (which is translated *Peter*).

43The next day Jesus wanted to go into Galilee, and he found Philip. Jesus said to him, "Follow me." 44Philip was from Bethsaida, the hometown of Andrew and Peter.

45Philip found Nathanael and said to him, "We have found the one Moses wrote about in the Law and the Prophets: Jesus, Joseph's son, from Nazareth."

46Nathanael responded, "Can anything from Nazareth be good?"

Philip said, "Come and see."

47Jesus saw Nathanael coming toward him and said about him, "Here is a genuine Israelite in whom there is no deceit."

48Nathanael asked him, "How do you know me?"

Jesus answered, "Before Philip called you, I saw you under the fig tree."
plied, "Rabbi, you are God's Son. You are the king of

d, "Do you believe because I told you that I saw you
You will see greater things than these! 51I assure you
eaven open and God's angels going up to heaven and
on the Human One."[d]

START THIS WEEK'S READING AT CHAPTER 2

Wedding at Cana

2 On the third day there was a wedding in Cana of Galilee. Jesus' mother was there, and 2Jesus and his disciples were also invited to the celebration. 3When the wine ran out, Jesus' mother said to him, "They don't have any wine."

[c]Or *Anointed One* [d]Or *Son of Man*

4 Jesus replied, "Woman, what does that have to do with me? My time hasn't come yet."

5 His mother told the servants, "Do whatever he tells you." 6 Nearby were six stone water jars used for the Jewish cleansing ritual, each able to hold about twenty or thirty gallons.

7 Jesus said to the servants, "Fill the jars with water," and they filled them to the brim. 8 Then he told them, "Now draw some from them and take it to the headwaiter," and they did. 9 The headwaiter tasted the water that had become wine. He didn't know where it came from, though the servants who had drawn the water knew.

The headwaiter called the groom 10 and said, "Everyone serves the good wine first. They bring out the second-rate wine only when the guests are drinking freely. You kept the good wine until now." 11 This was the first miraculous sign that Jesus did in Cana of Galilee. He revealed his glory, and his disciples believed in him.

12 After this, Jesus and his mother, his brothers, and his disciples went down to Capernaum and stayed there for a few days.

Jesus in Jerusalem at Passover

13 It was nearly time for the Jewish Passover, and Jesus went up to Jerusalem. 14 He found in the temple those who were selling cattle, sheep, and doves, as well as those involved in exchanging currency sitting there. 15 He made a whip from ropes and chased them all out of the temple, including the cattle and the sheep. He scattered the coins and overturned the tables of those who exchanged currency. 16 He said to the dove sellers, "Get these things out of here! Don't make my Father's house a place of business." 17 His disciples remembered that it is written, *Passion for your house consumes me.*[e]

18 Then the Jewish leaders asked him, "By what authority are you doing these things? What miraculous sign will you show us?"

19 Jesus answered, "Destroy this temple and in three days I'll raise it up."

20 The Jewish leaders replied, "It took forty-six years to build this temple, and you will raise it up in three days?" 21 But the temple Jesus was talking about was his body. 22 After he was raised from the dead, his disciples remembered what he had said, and they believed the scripture and the word that Jesus had spoken.

23 While Jesus was in Jerusalem for the Passover Festival, many believed in his name because they saw the miraculous signs that he did. 24 But Jesus didn't trust himself to them because he knew all people.

[e] Ps 69:9

John 2:25
25He didn't need anyone to tell him about human nature, for he knew
what human nature was.

Jesus and Nicodemus

3 There was a Pharisee named Nicodemus, a Jewish leader. 2He came
to Jesus at night and said to him, "Rabbi, we know that you are a
teacher who has come from God, for no one could do these miraculous
signs that you do unless God is with him."
3Jesus answered, "I assure you, unless someone is born anew,[f] it's not
possible to see God's kingdom."
4Nicodemus asked, "How is it possible for an adult to be born? It's impos-
sible to enter the mother's womb for a second time and be born, isn't it?"
5Jesus answered, "I assure you, unless someone is born of water and
the Spirit, it's not possible to enter God's kingdom. 6Whatever is born
of the flesh is flesh, and whatever is born of the Spirit is spirit. 7Don't
be surprised that I said to you, 'You must be born anew.' 8God's Spirit[g]
blows wherever it wishes. You hear its sound, but you don't know where
it comes from or where it is going. It's the same with everyone who is
born of the Spirit."
9Nicodemus said, "How are these things possible?"
10"Jesus answered, "You are a teacher of Israel and you don't know
these things? 11I assure you that we speak about what we know and
testify about what we have seen, but you don't receive our testimony.
12If I have told you about earthly things and you don't believe, how will
you believe if I tell you about heavenly things? 13No one has gone up
to heaven except the one who came down from heaven, the Human
One.[h] 14Just as Moses lifted up the snake in the wilderness, so must the
Human One[i] be lifted up 15so that everyone who believes in him will
have eternal life. 16God so loved the world that he gave his only Son, so
that everyone who believes in him won't perish but will have eternal
life. 17God didn't send his Son into the world to judge the world, but
that the world might be saved through him. 18Whoever believes in him
isn't judged; whoever doesn't believe in him is already judged, because
they don't believe in the name of God's only Son.
19"This is the basis for judgment: The light came into the world, and
people loved darkness more than the light, for their actions are evil.
20All who do wicked things hate the light and don't come to the light for
fear that their actions will be exposed to the light. 21Whoever does the
truth comes to the light so that it can be seen that their actions were
done in God."

[f]Or *from above* [g]Or *wind* [h]Or *Son of Man* [i]Or *Son of Man*

John's final witness

22 After this Jesus and his disciples went into Judea, where he spent
some time with them and was baptizing. 23 John was baptizing at Aenon
near Salem because there was a lot of water there, and people were coming
to him and being baptized. (24 John hadn't yet been thrown into prison.)

25 A debate started between John's disciples and a certain Jew about
cleansing rituals. 26 They came to John and said, "Rabbi, look! The man
who was with you across the Jordan, the one about whom you testified,
is baptizing and everyone is flocking to him."

27 John replied, "No one can receive anything unless it is given from
heaven. 28 You yourselves can testify that I said that I'm not the Christ
but that I'm the one sent before him. 29 The groom is the one who is
getting married. The friend of the groom stands close by and, when he
hears him, is overjoyed at the groom's voice. Therefore, my joy is now
complete. 30 He must increase and I must decrease. 31 The one who comes
from above is above all things. The one who is from the earth belongs
to the earth and speaks as one from the earth. The one who comes from
heaven is above all things. 32 He testifies to what he has seen and heard,
but no one accepts his testimony. 33 Whoever accepts his testimony con-
firms that God is true. 34 The one whom God sent speaks God's words
because God gives the Spirit generously. 35 The Father loves the Son
and gives everything into his hands. 36 Whoever believes in the Son has
eternal life. Whoever doesn't believe in the Son won't see life, but the
angry judgment of God remains on them."

Jesus leaves Judea

4 Jesus learned that the Pharisees had heard that he was making more
disciples and baptizing more than John (2 although Jesus' disciples
were baptizing, not Jesus himself). 3 Therefore, he left Judea and went
back to Galilee.

Jesus in Samaria

4 Jesus had to go through Samaria. 5 He came to a Samaritan city called
Sychar, which was near the land Jacob had given to his son Joseph.
6 Jacob's well was there. Jesus was tired from his journey, so he sat down
at the well. It was about noon.

7 A Samaritan woman came to the well to draw water. Jesus said to
her, "Give me some water to drink." 8 His disciples had gone into the city
to buy him some food.

9 The Samaritan woman asked, "Why do you, a Jewish man, ask for
something to drink from me, a Samaritan woman?" (Jews and Samaritans
didn't associate with each other.)

John 4:10

10 Jesus responded, "If you recognized God's gift and who is saying to you, 'Give me some water to drink,' you would be asking him and he would give you living water."

11 The woman said to him, "Sir, you don't have a bucket and the well is deep. Where would you get this living water? 12 You aren't greater than our father Jacob, are you? He gave this well to us, and he drank from it himself, as did his sons and his livestock."

13 Jesus answered, "Everyone who drinks this water will be thirsty again, 14 but whoever drinks from the water that I will give will never be thirsty again. The water that I give will become in those who drink it a spring of water that bubbles up into eternal life."

15 The woman said to him, "Sir, give me this water, so that I will never be thirsty and will never need to come here to draw water!"

16 Jesus said to her, "Go, get your husband, and come back here."

17 The woman replied, "I don't have a husband."

"You are right to say, 'I don't have a husband,'" Jesus answered. 18 "You've had five husbands, and the man you are with now isn't your husband. You've spoken the truth."

19 The woman said, "Sir, I see that you are a prophet. 20 Our ancestors worshipped on this mountain, but you and your people say that it is necessary to worship in Jerusalem."

21 Jesus said to her, "Believe me, woman, the time is coming when you and your people will worship the Father neither on this mountain nor in Jerusalem. 22 You and your people worship what you don't know; we worship what we know because salvation is from the Jews. 23 But the time is coming—and is here!—when true worshippers will worship in spirit and truth. The Father looks for those who worship him this way. 24 God is spirit, and it is necessary to worship God in spirit and truth."

25 The woman said, "I know that the Messiah is coming, the one who is called the Christ. When he comes, he will teach everything to us."

26 Jesus said to her, "I Am—the one who speaks with you."[j]

27 Just then, Jesus' disciples arrived and were shocked that he was talking with a woman. But no one asked, "What do you want?" or "Why are you talking with her?" 28 The woman put down her water jar and went into the city. She said to the people, 29 "Come and see a man who has told me everything I've done! Could this man be the Christ?" 30 They left the city and were on their way to see Jesus.

31 In the meantime the disciples spoke to Jesus, saying, "Rabbi, eat."

32 Jesus said to them, "I have food to eat that you don't know about."

33 The disciples asked each other, "Has someone brought him food?"

[j] Or *It is I, the one who speaks with you.*

34 Jesus said to them, "I am fed by doing the will of the one who sent
me and by completing his work. 35 Don't you have a saying, 'Four more
months and then it's time for harvest'? Look, I tell you: open your eyes
and notice that the fields are already ripe for the harvest. 36 Those who
harvest are receiving their pay and gathering fruit for eternal life so
that those who sow and those who harvest can celebrate together.
37 This is a true saying, that one sows and another harvests. 38 I have
sent you to harvest what you didn't work hard for; others worked hard,
and you will share in their hard work."

39 Many Samaritans in that city believed in Jesus because of the woman's word when she testified, "He told me everything I've ever done."
40 So when the Samaritans came to Jesus, they asked him to stay with
them, and he stayed there two days. 41 Many more believed because of
his word, 42 and they said to the woman, "We no longer believe because
of what you said, for we have heard for ourselves and know that this
one is truly the savior of the world."

Jesus arrives in Galilee

43 After two days Jesus left for Galilee. (44 Jesus himself had testified
that prophets have no honor in their own country.) 45 When he came
to Galilee, the Galileans welcomed him because they had seen all the
things he had done in Jerusalem during the festival, for they also had
been at the festival.

Jesus' second miraculous sign in Galilee

46 He returned to Cana in Galilee where he had turned the water into
wine. In Capernaum there was a certain royal official whose son was
sick. 47 When he heard that Jesus was coming from Judea to Galilee, he
went out to meet him and asked Jesus if he would come and heal his
son, for his son was about to die. 48 Jesus said to him, "Unless you see
miraculous signs and wonders, you won't believe."

49 The royal official said to him, "Lord, come before my son dies."

50 Jesus replied, "Go home. Your son lives." The man believed the word
that Jesus spoke to him and set out for his home.

51 While he was on his way, his servants were already coming to meet
him. They said, "Your son lives!" 52 So he asked them at what time his
son had started to get better. And they said, "The fever left him yester-
day at about one o'clock in the afternoon." 53 Then the father realized
that this was the hour when Jesus had said to him, "Your son lives."
And he and his entire household believed in Jesus. 54 This was the second miraculous sign Jesus did while going from Judea to Galilee.

John 5:1

Sabbath healing

5 After this there was a Jewish festival, and Jesus went up to Jerusalem. 2In Jerusalem near the Sheep Gate in the north city wall is a pool with the Aramaic name Bethsaida. It had five covered porches, 3and a crowd of people who were sick, blind, lame, and paralyzed sat there.[k] 5A certain man was there who had been sick for thirty-eight years. 6When Jesus saw him lying there, knowing that he had already been there a long time, he asked him, "Do you want to get well?"

7The sick man answered him, "Sir,[l] I don't have anyone who can put me in the water when it is stirred up. When I'm trying to get to it, someone else has gotten in ahead of me."

8Jesus said to him, "Get up! Pick up your mat and walk." 9Immediately the man was well, and he picked up his mat and walked. Now that day was the Sabbath.

10The Jewish leaders said to the man who had been healed, "It's the Sabbath; you aren't allowed to carry your mat."

11He answered, "The man who made me well said to me, 'Pick up your mat and walk.'"

12They inquired, "Who is this man who said to you, 'Pick it up and walk'?" 13The man who had been cured didn't know who it was, because Jesus had slipped away from the crowd gathered there.

14Later Jesus found him in the temple and said, "See! You have been made well. Don't sin anymore in case something worse happens to you." 15The man went and proclaimed to the Jewish leaders that Jesus was the man who had made him well.

16As a result, the Jewish leaders were harassing Jesus, since he had done these things on the Sabbath. 17Jesus replied, "My Father is still working, and I am working too." 18For this reason the Jewish leaders wanted even more to kill him—not only because he was doing away with the Sabbath but also because he called God his own Father, thereby making himself equal with God.

Work of the Father and the Son

19Jesus responded to the Jewish leaders, "I assure you that the Son can't do anything by himself except what he sees the Father doing. Whatever the Father does, the Son does likewise. 20The Father loves the Son and shows him everything that he does. He will show him greater works than these so that you will marvel. 21As the Father raises the dead and gives life, so too does the Son give life to whomever he wishes.

[k]Critical editions of the Gk New Testament do not include the following addition *waiting for the water to move. [4]Sometimes an angel would come down to the pool and stir up the water. Then the first one going into the water after it had been stirred up was cured of any sickness.* [l]Or *Lord*

[22]The Father doesn't judge anyone, but he has given all judgment to
the Son [23]so that everyone will honor the Son just as they honor the
Father. Whoever doesn't honor the Son doesn't honor the Father who
sent him.

[24]"I assure you that whoever hears my word and believes in the one
who sent me has eternal life and won't come under judgment but has
passed from death into life.

[25]"I assure you that the time is coming—and is here!—when the dead
will hear the voice of God's Son, and those who hear it will live. [26]Just as
the Father has life in himself, so he has granted the Son to have life in
himself. [27]He gives the Son authority to judge, because he is the Human
One.[m] [28]Don't be surprised by this, because the time is coming when all
who are in their graves will hear his voice. [29]Those who did good things
will come out into the resurrection of life, and those who did wicked
things into the resurrection of judgment. [30]I can't do anything by myself. Whatever I hear, I judge, and my judgment is just. I don't seek my
own will but the will of the one who sent me.

Witnesses to Jesus

[31]"If I testify about myself, my testimony isn't true. [32]There is someone else who testifies about me, and I know his testimony about me
is true. [33]You sent a delegation to John, and he testified to the truth.
[34]Although I don't accept human testimony, I say these things so that
you can be saved. [35]John was a burning and shining lamp, and, at least
for a while, you were willing to celebrate in his light.

[36]"I have a witness greater than John's testimony. The Father has
given me works to do so that I might complete them. These works I do
testify about me that the Father sent me. [37]And the Father who sent me
testifies about me. You have never even heard his voice or seen his form,
[38]and you don't have his word dwelling with you because you don't believe the one whom he has sent. [39]Examine the scriptures, since you
think that in them you have eternal life. They also testify about me,
[40]yet you don't want to come to me so that you can have life.

[41]"I don't accept praise from people, [42]but I know you, that you don't
have God's love in you. [43]I have come in my Father's name, and you
don't receive me. If others come in their own name, you receive them.
[44]How can you believe when you receive praise from each other but
don't seek the praise that comes from the only God?

[45]"Don't think that I will accuse you before the Father. Your accuser is
Moses, the one in whom your hope rests. [46]If you believed Moses, you

[m]Or *Son of Man*

would believe me, because Moses wrote about me. 47 If you don't believe
the writings of Moses, how will you believe my words?"

Chapter Three

The "I AM" Sayings of Jesus

But Moses said to God, "If I now come to the Israelites and say to them, 'The God of your ancestors has sent me to you,' they are going to ask me, 'What's this God's name?' What am I supposed to say to them?" God said to Moses, "I Am Who I Am. So say to the Israelites, 'I Am has sent me to you.'" (Exodus 3:13-14)

"Your father Abraham was overjoyed that he would see my day. He saw it and was happy." "You aren't even 50 years old!" the Jewish opposition replied. "How can you say that you have seen Abraham?" "I assure you," Jesus replied, "before Abraham was, I Am." (John 8:56-58)

3

THE "I AM" SAYINGS OF JESUS

As we continue the study of Jesus in the Gospel of John, I remind you that John writes so that we might understand who Jesus Christ is and the ways in which he offers life to those who believe in him.

Theologians speak about the category of theology that deals with the identity of Jesus as *Christology*, the study of Christ. In theology, a distinction is made between a low Christology and a high Christology. A low Christology focuses on Jesus' humanity—on Jesus as a teacher, leader, and prophet. A high Christology focuses on Christ's divinity—his divine nature, his oneness with God. Ideally in Christian theology, we have a balance of low and high Christology. No book of the New Testament has a higher Christology than John.

We now turn our attention to what are often referred to as the "I AM" sayings of Jesus that are recorded in John. These are statements in which two simple Greek words, *ego eimi*, are heard on the lips of Jesus. These two Greek words can mean a variety of things. They can be used to say "It is I," or "I am he," or "I exist," or most commonly "I am," as when my wife says, "Are you hungry?" and I say, "I am." These are such commonplace words that we might read them in John and not really think anything about them.

Yet, as with so much in John's Gospel, there is more here than meets the eye—in fact, much more. To see why these two words are important in John, it is helpful to go back to Exodus 3. The Israelites were enslaved in Egypt. Moses was living in the Sinai desert, tending the flock of his father-in-law. One day he saw a bush burning in the wilderness. Approaching to investigate, he heard a voice from the bush calling his name: "Moses, Moses!" Here's what the voice said next:

> "Don't come any closer! Take off your sandals, because you are standing on holy ground. . . . I am the God of your father, Abraham's God, Isaac's God, and Jacob's God." Moses hid his face because he was afraid to look at God. (Exodus 3:5-6)

The voice went on to say, in effect, "I've heard the suffering of my people Israel, and I'm going to set them free from their captivity in Egypt." God then called Moses to go to Egypt and lead the Israelites to freedom. Moses responded:

> "If I now come to the Israelites and say to them, 'The God of your ancestors has sent me to you,' they are going to ask me, 'What's this God's name?' What am I supposed to say to them?" (v.13)

Remember, Moses had grown up in a polytheistic culture and was still living in one, so he was familiar with many gods. He wanted to know which god was speaking to him and calling him to go liberate the Israelites. If he knew the god's name, then he could call upon that god and ask for blessings and intercessions. Here's the important passage as it relates to John's account of the "I AM" sayings of Jesus:

> God said to Moses, "I Am Who I Am." So say to the Israelites, "I Am has sent me to you." (v.14)

God's name, given to Moses, is I Am. What kind of name is that? In Hebrew, the word that's translated as *I Am Who I Am*[1] is the Hebrew word *Yahweh* or, as it is sometimes pronounced, *Jehovah.* Throughout the Old Testament this is the personal name for God, God's covenant name. Still, what an odd name God has chosen to reveal to Moses. By revealing this name, I believe God was saying, "I am being itself!" Or, "I am the source of existence (or life) itself!" Moses asked, "Who are you?" God replied, "I Am."

In other words, everything that exists is contingent upon God for its existence. Every molecule, every atom, every subatomic particle, every cell in your body derives its energy and existence from God. God defines what Being is. This is why, at the burning bush, God said his name was I Am. It's why Paul could say, "In God we live, move, and exist" (Acts 17:28a). And it's why, centuries later, existential theologian Paul Tillich wrote that God is "the Ground of our being."[2]

Every molecule, every atom, every subatomic particle, every cell in your body derives its energy and existence from God.

I Am (*Yahweh*) thus became the personal name for God throughout the Scriptures. The name was so revered that by the third or fourth century before Christ, if not earlier, faithful Jews would not even speak what came to be known with reverence as "the Name" (in Hebrew, *ha shem*). When you saw the word *Yahweh* in the text, you would say another word that was less revered: *Adonai. Adonai* was the Hebrew word for "Lord," but it wasn't God's personal name. In most translations of the Old Testament, when you find the word *LORD* (in small caps), behind that word is the Hebrew word *Yahweh*, the personal name for God. It appears hundreds of times in your Bible. If you find the word *Lord*, not in small caps, it is translated from the word *Adonai.*

JESUS CLAIMS "I AM"

Let's return to the Gospel of John, chapter 8. As you read, keep in mind that Abraham is said to have lived somewhere between 1,600 and 1,800 years before the birth of Christ. In John 8:56-58, Jesus spoke to the Jewish leaders:

> "Your father Abraham was overjoyed that he would see my day. He saw it and was happy." "You aren't even 50 years old!" the Jewish opposition replied. "How can you say that you have seen Abraham?" "I assure you," Jesus replied, "before Abraham was, *I Am* [emphasis added]."

The Jewish leaders, upon hearing Jesus say this, picked up stones to kill him. This was the Old Testament punishment for blasphemy. The blasphemy wasn't only in claiming to have been around before the time of Abraham, but the uttering of words that seemed to associate Jesus with Yahweh.

In John's Gospel, the "blasphemous" phrase "*I Am*" is uttered by Jesus over and over again. In some cases, as with John 8:58, the words stand alone: "Before Abraham was, I Am." We see this in John 8:24: "If you don't believe that I Am, you will die in your sins." We see it in John 8:28: "When the Human One is lifted up, then you will know that I Am." In John 6:20, when Jesus walked on water to meet his disciples in the boat, he said to them, "I Am. Don't be afraid." (In Chapter 5 of this book, we'll consider Jesus' use of these words as the soldiers came to arrest him.)

These uses of "I Am" prepare the reader for the conversation Philip and Jesus have in John 14:8-9: "Philip said to Jesus, 'Lord, show us the Father; that will be enough for us.' Jesus replied, 'Don't you know me, Philip, even after I have been with you all this time? Whoever has seen me has seen the Father.'"

THE "I AM" SAYINGS

Recognizing the way in which John uses *ego eimi* (or records Jesus' use of the words), we can see that some of these uses belong to a category of sayings that is slightly different from what we just read, but which John likely intends for us to see as similar to each other. In the uses of "I Am" above, the phrase stands alone: "Before Abraham was, I Am." But there are other sayings in which Jesus uses the words "I Am" followed by a metaphor meant to further connect Jesus with God, and which describes how those who believe in Jesus "will have life in his name" (John 20:31). The sayings in this second category are traditionally known as the "I AM" sayings of Jesus.

Here are the seven "I AM" sayings that we find in John, each a definitive statement from Jesus in which a metaphor is used to describe how Jesus gives life to those who believe in his name:

"I am the bread of life." (6:35)
"I am the light of the world." (8:12)
"I am the gate of the sheep." (10:7; cf. v.9)
"I am the good shepherd." (10:11, 14)
"I am the resurrection and the life." (11:25)
"I am the way, the truth, and the life." (14:6)
"I am the true vine." (15:1; cf. v.5)

As with the seven miraculous signs described in the previous chapter, I'd like to focus on just two of these statements and then invite you to consider the significance of the others on your own.

"I AM THE BREAD OF LIFE." (6:35)

As we prepare to examine Jesus' first "I AM" statement, "I am the bread of life," let's first consider the context of the statement. Nearly the entire sixth chapter of John is devoted to the feeding of the multitudes with just a few loaves of bread and a couple of fish (the only miracle of Jesus that appears in all four Gospels) and the subsequent dialogue Jesus had with the crowds. True to form, John's telling of this story is about more than the miracle of how Jesus fed thousands with a few loaves and fish; the miracle is a sign pointing to who Jesus is and how he gives life, and John provides multiple clues by which we can see the deeper meaning.

In John 6:4 we read, "It was nearly time for Passover, the Jewish festival." This reference is the first clue. The Passover is the annual celebration of God's deliverance of the Israelites from slavery in Egypt. The celebration includes a festive meal in which families reenact the events of Israel's last night as slaves in Egypt and of their miraculous deliverance. You'll recall that God sent plague after plague upon the Egyptians to convince them to release the Israelite slaves. The last plague God announced to Moses would be the death of the firstborn children in Egypt. The plague would be so onerous that the Egyptians would beg the Israelites to leave.

On the night of the last plague, the Israelites were to slaughter and roast a lamb, then mark their doorposts with the blood of the lamb. The angel of death passed through Egypt to claim the lives of the firstborn, but upon seeing the blood of the lamb on the doorposts, death passed over the homes of the Israelites. Once the Egyptians discovered what had happened, they demanded that the Israelites leave their land.

The meal the Israelites ate that night before the plague included lamb and unleavened bread. From that time forward a meal including bread and lamb and wine would be an annual celebration of God's deliverance of his people. Eating the Passover Seder meal is a way for all Jews to reenact and become a part of that story and to claim it as *their* story.

With this in mind, let's turn back to John 6:4, where John has begun telling about the feeding of the multitudes. By referring to the Passover at the beginning of his account, John invites us to see Jesus' miracle and subsequent words against the backdrop of the Passover.

The second clue John offers has to do with the bread itself. When Jesus multiplies the loaves and then says, "I am the bread of life," John is encouraging us to think of other occurrences of bread in the Old Testament. There are over two hundred references to bread in the Old Testament, and these provide rich possibilities for deeper meaning in Jesus' claim to be the bread of life.

One prominent reference to bread in the Old Testament is the manna God sent to feed the Israelites every morning as they wandered in the wilderness for forty years, following their release from captivity in Egypt. This bread is specifically mentioned in John 6:31-35, where we read a comment from some people in the crowd, along with Jesus' response:

> "Our ancestors ate manna in the wilderness, just as it is written, *He gave them bread from heaven to eat.*" Jesus told them, "I assure you, it wasn't Moses who gave the bread from heaven to you, but my Father gives you the true bread from heaven. The bread of God is the one who comes down from heaven and gives life to the world." They said, "Sir, give us this bread all the time!" Jesus replied, "I am the bread of life. Whoever comes to me will never go hungry, and whoever believes in me will never be thirsty."

In the Synoptic Gospels, Jesus shared the Passover Seder with the disciples as his Last Supper just before his arrest. There he gave new meaning to the bread and wine used at the Passover, saying of the bread, "This is my body" (Mark 14:22) and of the wine, "This is my blood" (Mark 14:24). The meal becomes for Christians what the Passover is for Jews, a meal in which we remember our defining story: that God came to us in Jesus Christ, who gave himself to save and deliver humanity from sin and death. In the meal, Christians become a part of the story, participating in Christ's story and in his saving work.

John does not recount Jesus' words at the Last Supper, reinterpreting the bread and wine in this way. (We'll see why in Chapter 5 of this book.) But John knows about the Eucharist and uses its symbolism in the story of the transformation of water into wine, and here in Jesus' words about being the bread of life. In both cases, anchoring the story and words in the Eucharist allows John to reveal the deeper meaning of Holy Communion. We see that clearly in John 6:53-56, where Jesus says,

> "I assure you, unless you eat the flesh of the Human One and drink his blood, you have no life in you. Whoever eats my flesh and drinks my blood has eternal life, and I will raise them up at

> the last day. My flesh is true food and my blood is true drink. Whoever eats my flesh and drinks my blood remains in me and I in them."

In his words, "I am the bread of life," Jesus draws from the Passover seder and the manna by which God sustained the Israelites in the wilderness. He does so to point to the deliverance he will bring by his death, and the way ongoing belief in him sustains his disciples. The Eucharistic meal encompasses both of these ideas.

But there is likely much more. Bread, for ancient people and still for many around the world, is an essential food of life. For most people throughout history, bread has been a part of every meal. The Latin word for breaking bread is *companere*, from which we have our word *companion*. Bread sustains but also binds people together.

For most people throughout history, bread has been a part of every meal. . . . Bread sustains but also binds people together.

Some years ago I spoke with a master baker about the history of bread. He noted, "Bread has always been the center of meals throughout history. It's something that I don't think anything could take the place of. It's a food source, it's a nutrient, but I think in a larger sense that it is a way to bring the community together. I guess in a way that other foods aren't shared, bread is usually something that is broken and shared."

When Jesus said "I am the bread of life," he was speaking about both of these ideas—spiritual nutrition or sustenance and bringing people together in community. New Testament scholar C. K. Barrett wrote, "Both [the story of feeding the multitudes] and the discourse are about the bread by which men live, without which they will die."[3]

Our most basic need as human beings is for food ("bread") and water as psychologist Abraham Maslow recognized in his hierarchy of human needs, first written about in 1954. Maslow placed them as our most basic need; we cannot survive without them. And so Jesus had said, "I am the bread of life. Whoever comes to me will never go hungry, and whoever believes in me will never be thirsty" (18:35). In other words, Jesus is the source of life, our spiritual sustenance.

Holy Communion is a means by which Christians recognize Christ as the bread of life, participate in his story, and invite him, both spiritually and physically, into our lives through the eating of the bread and drinking of the wine. St. Ignatius of Antioch, a first-century believer mentored by John, wrote in his Epistle to the Ephesians that the Eucharist is the "medicine of immortality and the antidote" to death.[4]

Jesus is also the bread that brings people together. When we speak of the Lord's Supper as Holy Communion, we are referring to the way this meal is meant to bring us into communion with God and with one another. When we break bread together, we are bound together. There's an old hymn that says, "Blest be the tie that binds our hearts in Christian love."[5] That's what Jesus does. Paul expressed it another way in 1 Corinthians 10:17: "Since there is one loaf of bread, we who are many are one body, because we all share the one loaf of bread."

"I AM THE LIGHT OF THE WORLD." (8:12)

The second "I AM" saying of Jesus that we will look at is expressed in this way: "Jesus spoke to the people again, saying, 'I am the light of the world. Whoever follows me won't walk in darkness but will have the light of life'" (John 8:12).

The context of this passage may be important in appreciating the statement. We read in John 7 that Jesus went to Jerusalem for the Festival of Sukkot. *Sukkot* is a Hebrew word meaning huts or booths; hence, the celebration is often called the Festival of Booths. This is a fall harvest festival in which the people erected (and Jews to this day continue to erect) tents (or temporary outside structures) to remember Israel's forty years of wandering in the wilderness, a time in which the people lived in tents or "booths."

The forty-year period is described in the Book of Exodus: "The LORD [Yahweh] went in front of them during the day in a column of cloud to guide them and at night in a column of lightning to give them light. This way they could travel during the day and at night" (Exodus 13:21).

In the time of Jesus, on the first night of the Festival of Sukkot, four giant lampstands seventy-five feet tall, each with four golden bowls at the top, were erected in the Court of the Women at the Temple. The bowls were filled with oil, and multiple wicks made of fabric were inserted into the bowls and lit. It was said that the light from these lampstands dramatically illuminated Jerusalem. These lamps were visible reminders of the column of light by which God guided the Israelites and reassured them as they sojourned in the wilderness.

It was at this festival, in the Temple courts where the lampstands stood, that Jesus made this "I AM" saying: "I am the light of the world. Whoever follows me won't walk in darkness but will have the light of life." In framing the story this way, John wants us to understand that Jesus came to guide those who believe in him through the darkness. He came to dispel the darkness. He came to be our light in the midst of the darkness.

As with the "bread of life," this "I AM" saying draws upon so many Old Testament Scriptures. We can find 180 or more references to light in the Old Testament, many of which may have been behind Jesus' "light of the world" statement. Psalm 27:1 proclaims, "The

Lord [Yahweh] is my light and my salvation. Should I fear anyone?" In Psalm 104:2, the psalmist sings to God, "You wear light like a robe." There are also the beautiful words of Psalm 139:11-12.

> If I said, "The darkness will definitely hide me;
> the light will become night around me,"
> even then the darkness isn't too dark for you!
> Nighttime would shine bright as day,
> because darkness is the same as light to you!

The prophets repeatedly speak of God bringing light to the people, as with the memorable words of Isaiah 9:2: "The people walking in darkness have seen a great light. On those living in a pitch-dark land, light has dawned." The early church saw in this passage a prophetic word about Jesus. Isaiah 60:19 points to a time when "the sun will no longer be your light by day, nor will the moon shine for illumination by night; the Lord will be your everlasting light; your God will be your glory."

Both in Scripture and in literature from the Dead Sea Scrolls, written just before the time of Christ, we find that themes of darkness and light were prominent in Judaism. Darkness represents spiritual blindness, lost-ness, and also evil. In John, when we believe in Jesus our eyes are opened, and suddenly we see ourselves and the world in his light.

In the Synoptic Gospels, the light metaphor shifts. Jesus does not say, "I am the light of the world" but instead says to his disciples, "You are the light of the world. A city on top of a hill can't be hidden. . . . Let your light shine before people, so they can see the good things you do and praise your Father who is in heaven" (Matthew 5:14, 16).

In the Synoptic Gospels . . . Jesus does not say, "I am the light of the world" but instead says to his disciples, "You are the light of the world."

Both statements are true, and at our Christmas Eve candlelight services, described earlier, we always link the two together. We light the Christ candle in the midst of the darkened room, showing that Jesus is the light of the world. Then we take the Christ candle and light all our candles from it, signifying that our lives have received the light of Christ. In doing so, we remember that we are called to leave the candlelight service and take the light of Christ to others.

Light and life—these two themes are found throughout the Gospel of John, and they reflect what John wants his readers to understand. Jesus lights our lives and the world, and he gives life to all people. These themes are captured memorably in the first two "I AM" sayings of Jesus: "I am the bread of life" and "I am the light of the world."

Lord Jesus, when I look at you I believe I am seeing the Father. I know that I need more than bread to live. I need you and the love, mercy, and life that you give. Be the bread of life for me. Sustain me and feed my soul. Be my light and dispel the darkness in my life. May your light so shine in me that others might see you through me. Amen.

The Gospel of John: Part Three

John 6–11 (CEB)

In John chapters 6–11 you will read additional stories of "miraculous signs" and many of the "I AM" sayings of Jesus.

START THIS WEEK'S READING AT CHAPTER 6

, because Moses wrote about me. 47If you don't believe
Moses, how will you believe my words?"

Feeding of the five thousand

6 After this Jesus went across the Galilee Sea (that is, the Tiberias
Sea). 2A large crowd followed him, because they had seen the miraculous signs he had done among the sick. 3Jesus went up a mountain
and sat there with his disciples. 4It was nearly time for Passover, the
Jewish festival.
5Jesus looked up and saw the large crowd coming toward him. He
asked Philip, "Where will we buy food to feed these people?" 6Jesus said
this to test him, for he already knew what he was going to do.
7Philip replied, "More than a half year's salary[n] worth of food wouldn't
be enough for each person to have even a little bit."
8One of his disciples, Andrew, Simon Peter's brother, said, 9"A youth
here has five barley loaves and two fish. But what good is that for a
crowd like this?"
10Jesus said, "Have the people sit down." There was plenty of grass
there. They sat down, about five thousand of them. 11Then Jesus took
the bread. When he had given thanks, he distributed it to those who
were sitting there. He did the same with the fish, each getting as much
as they wanted. 12When they had plenty to eat, he said to his disciples,
"Gather up the leftover pieces, so that nothing will be wasted." 13So they
gathered them and filled twelve baskets with the pieces of the five barley loaves that had been left over by those who had eaten.
14When the people saw that he had done a miraculous sign, they said,
"This is truly the prophet who is coming into the world." 15Jesus understood that they were about to come and force him to be their king, so
he took refuge again, alone on a mountain.

Jesus walks on water

16When evening came, Jesus' disciples went down to the lake. 17They
got into a boat and were crossing the lake to Capernaum. It was already
getting dark and Jesus hadn't come to them yet. 18The water was getting rough because a strong wind was blowing. 19When the wind had
driven them out for about three or four miles, they saw Jesus walking
on the water. He was approaching the boat and they were afraid. 20He
said to them, "I Am.[o] Don't be afraid." 21Then they wanted to take him
into the boat, and just then the boat reached the land where they had
been heading.

[n] Or *two hundred denaria* [o] Or *It is I.*

22 The next day the crowd that remained on the other side of the lake
realized that only one boat had been there. They knew Jesus hadn't gone
with his disciples, but that the disciples had gone alone. 23 Some boats
came from Tiberias, near the place where they had eaten the bread over
which the Lord had given thanks. 24 When the crowd saw that neither
Jesus nor his disciples were there, they got into the boats and came to
Capernaum looking for Jesus. 25 When they found him on the other side
of the lake, they asked him, "Rabbi, when did you get here?"

Bread of life

26 Jesus replied, "I assure you that you are looking for me not because
you saw miraculous signs but because you ate all the food you wanted.
27 Don't work for the food that doesn't last but for the food that endures
for eternal life, which the Human One[p] will give you. God the Father
has confirmed him as his agent to give life."

28 They asked, "What must we do in order to accomplish what God
requires?"

29 Jesus replied, "This is what God requires, that you believe in him
whom God sent."

30 They asked, "What miraculous sign will you do, that we can see and
believe you? What will you do? 31 Our ancestors ate manna in the wilderness, just as it is written, *He gave them bread from heaven to eat*."[q]

32 Jesus told them, "I assure you, it wasn't Moses who gave the bread
from heaven to you, but my Father gives you the true bread from
heaven. 33 The bread of God is the one who comes down from heaven
and gives life to the world."

34 They said, "Sir,[r] give us this bread all the time!"

35 Jesus replied, "I am the bread of life. Whoever comes to me will never
go hungry, and whoever believes in me will never be thirsty. 36 But I told
you that you have seen me and still don't believe. 37 Everyone whom the
Father gives to me will come to me, and I won't send away anyone who
comes to me. 38 I have come down from heaven not to do my will, but
the will of him who sent me. 39 This is the will of the one who sent me,
that I won't lose anything he has given me, but I will raise it up at the
last day. 40 This is my Father's will: that all who see the Son and believe
in him will have eternal life, and I will raise them up at the last day."

41 The Jewish opposition grumbled about him because he said, "I am
the bread that came down from heaven."

42 They asked, "Isn't this Jesus, Joseph's son, whose mother and father
we know? How can he now say, 'I have come down from heaven'?"

[p] Or *Son of Man* [q] Ps 78:24 [r] Or *Lord*

John 6:43

43 Jesus responded, “Don’t grumble among yourselves. 44 No one can come to me unless they are drawn to me by the Father who sent me, and I will raise them up at the last day. 45 It is written in the Prophets, And they *will all be taught by God.*[s] Everyone who has listened to the Father and learned from him comes to me. 46 No one has seen the Father except the one who is from God. He has seen the Father. 47 I assure you, whoever believes has eternal life. 48 I am the bread of life. 49 Your ancestors ate manna in the wilderness and they died. 50 This is the bread that comes down from heaven so that whoever eats from it will never die. 51 I am the living bread that came down from heaven. Whoever eats this bread will live forever, and the bread that I will give for the life of the world is my flesh.”

52 Then the Jews debated among themselves, asking, “How can this man give us his flesh to eat?”

53 Jesus said to them, “I assure you, unless you eat the flesh of the Human One[t] and drink his blood, you have no life in you. 54 Whoever eats my flesh and drinks my blood has eternal life, and I will raise them up at the last day. 55 My flesh is true food and my blood is true drink. 56 Whoever eats my flesh and drinks my blood remains in me and I in them. 57 As the living Father sent me, and I live because of the Father, so whoever eats me lives because of me. 58 This is the bread that came down from heaven. It isn’t like the bread your ancestors ate, and then they died. Whoever eats this bread will live forever.” 59 Jesus said these things while he was teaching in the synagogue in Capernaum.

60 Many of his disciples who heard this said, “This message is harsh. Who can hear it?”

61 Jesus knew that the disciples were grumbling about this and he said to them, “Does this offend you? 62 What if you were to see the Human One[u] going up where he was before? 63 The Spirit is the one who gives life and the flesh doesn’t help at all. The words I have spoken to you are spirit and life. 64 Yet some of you don’t believe.” Jesus knew from the beginning who wouldn’t believe and the one who would betray him. 65 He said, “For this reason I said to you that none can come to me unless the Father enables them to do so.” 66 At this, many of his disciples turned away and no longer accompanied him.

67 Jesus asked the Twelve, “Do you also want to leave?”

68 Simon Peter answered, “Lord, where would we go? You have the words of eternal life. 69 We believe and know that you are God’s holy one.”

70 Jesus replied, “Didn’t I choose you twelve? Yet one of you is a devil.”

[s]Isa 54:13 [t]Or *Son of Man* [u]Or *Son of Man*

[71]He was speaking of Judas, Simon Iscariot's son, for he, one of the
Twelve, was going to betray him.

Jesus goes to Jerusalem

7 After this Jesus traveled throughout Galilee. He didn't want to travel
in Judea, because the Jewish authorities wanted to kill him. [2]When
it was almost time for the Jewish Festival of Booths, [3]Jesus' brothers
said to him, "Leave Galilee. Go to Judea so that your disciples can see
the amazing works that you do. [4]Those who want to be known publicly
don't do things secretly. Since you can do these things, show yourself
to the world." [5]His brothers said this because even they didn't believe
in him.

[6]Jesus replied, "For you, anytime is fine. But my time hasn't come
yet. [7]The world can't hate you. It hates me, though, because I testify
that its works are evil. [8]You go up to the festival. I'm not going to this
one because my time hasn't yet come." [9]Having said this, he stayed in
Galilee. [10]However, after his brothers left for the festival, he went too—
not openly but in secret.

[11]The Jewish leaders were looking for Jesus at the festival. They kept
asking, "Where is he?" [12]The crowds were murmuring about him. "He's
a good man," some said, but others were saying, "No, he tricks the
people." [13]No one spoke about him publicly, though, for fear of the Jewish authorities.

Jesus teaches in the temple

[14]Halfway through the festival, Jesus went up to the temple and
started to teach. [15]Astonished, the Jewish leaders asked, "He's never
been taught! How has he mastered the Law?"

[16]Jesus responded, "My teaching isn't mine but comes from the one
who sent me. [17]Whoever wants to do God's will can tell whether my
teaching is from God or whether I speak on my own. [18]Those who speak
on their own seek glory for themselves. Those who seek the glory of
him who sent me are people of truth; there's no falsehood in them.
[19]Didn't Moses give you the Law? Yet none of you keep the Law. Why
do you want to kill me?"

[20]The crowd answered, "You have a demon. Who wants to kill you?"

[21]Jesus replied, "I did one work, and you were all astonished. [22]Be-
cause Moses gave you the commandment about circumcision (although
it wasn't Moses but the patriarchs), you circumcise a man on the Sabbath. [23]If a man can be circumcised on the Sabbath without breaking
Moses' Law, why are you angry with me because I made an entire man

well on the Sabbath? 24Don't judge according to appearances. Judge with right judgment."

25Some people from Jerusalem said, "Isn't he the one they want to kill? 26Here he is, speaking in public, yet they aren't saying anything to him. Could it be that our leaders actually think he is the Christ? 27We know where he is from, but when the Christ comes, no one will know where he is from."

28While Jesus was teaching in the temple, he exclaimed, "You know me and where I am from. I haven't come on my own. The one who sent me is true, and you don't know him. 29I know him because I am from him and he sent me." 30So they wanted to seize Jesus, but they couldn't because his time hadn't yet come.

31Many from that crowd believed in Jesus. They said, "When the Christ comes, will he do more miraculous signs than this man does?" 32The Pharisees heard the crowd whispering such things about Jesus, and the chief priests and Pharisees sent guards to arrest him.

33Therefore, Jesus said, "I'm still with you for a little while before I go to the one who sent me. 34You will look for me, but you won't find me, and where I am you can't come."

35The Jewish opposition asked each other, "Where does he intend to go that we can't find him? Surely he doesn't intend to go where our people have been scattered and are living among the Greeks! He isn't going to teach the Greeks, is he? 36What does he mean when he says, 'You will look for me, but you won't find me, and where I am you can't come'?"

37On the last and most important day of the festival, Jesus stood up and shouted,

"All who are thirsty should come to me!
38All who believe in me should drink!
As the scriptures said concerning me,[v]
Rivers of living water will flow out from within him."

39Jesus said this concerning the Spirit. Those who believed in him would soon receive the Spirit, but they hadn't experienced the Spirit yet since Jesus hadn't yet been glorified.

40When some in the crowd heard these words, they said, "This man is truly the prophet." 41Others said, "He's the Christ." But others said, "The Christ can't come from Galilee, can he? 42Didn't the scripture say that the Christ comes from David's family and from Bethlehem, David's village?" 43So the crowd was divided over Jesus. 44Some wanted to arrest him, but no one grabbed him.

[v] Or *Whoever is thirsty should come to me and drink. Whoever believes in me, just as the scriptures said,* rivers of living water will flow out from within them.

45 The guards returned to the chief priests and Pharisees, who asked,
"Why didn't you bring him?"
46 The guards answered, "No one has ever spoken the way he does."
47 The Pharisees replied, "Have you too been deceived? 48 Have any of
the leaders believed in him? Has any Pharisee? 49 No, only this crowd,
which doesn't know the Law. And they are under God's curse!"
50 Nicodemus, who was one of them and had come to Jesus earlier,
said, 51 "Our Law doesn't judge someone without first hearing him and
learning what he is doing, does it?"
52 They answered him, "You are not from Galilee too, are you? Look it
up and you will see that the prophet doesn't come from Galilee."

Pharisees test Jesus

53 They each went to their own homes,
8 And Jesus went to the Mount of Olives. 2 Early in the morning
he returned to the temple. All the people gathered around him,
and he sat down and taught them. 3 The legal experts and Pharisees
brought a woman caught in adultery. Placing her in the center of
the group, 4 they said to Jesus, "Teacher, this woman was caught in
the act of committing adultery. 5 In the Law, Moses commanded us
to stone women like this. What do you say?" 6 They said this to test
him, because they wanted a reason to bring an accusation against
him. Jesus bent down and wrote on the ground with his finger.
7 They continued to question him, so he stood up and replied, "Whoever hasn't sinned should throw the first stone." 8 Bending down
again, he wrote on the ground. 9 Those who heard him went away,
one by one, beginning with the elders. Finally, only Jesus and the
woman were left in the middle of the crowd.
10 Jesus stood up and said to her, "Woman, where are they? Is there
no one to condemn you?"
11 She said, "No one, sir."[w]
Jesus said, "Neither do I condemn you. Go, and from now on, don't
sin anymore."[x]

Jesus continues to teach in the temple

12 Jesus spoke to the people again, saying, "I am the light of the world.
Whoever follows me won't walk in darkness but will have the light
of life."

[w] Or *Lord* [x] Critical editions of the Gk New Testament do not contain 7:53–8:11.

John 8:13

13 Then the Pharisees said to him, "Because you are testifying about
yourself, your testimony isn't valid."

14 Jesus replied, "Even if I testify about myself, my testimony is true,
since I know where I came from and where I'm going. You don't know
where I come from or where I'm going. 15 You judge according to human
standards, but I judge no one. 16 Even if I do judge, my judgment is truth-
ful, because I'm not alone. My judgments come from me and from the
Father who sent me. 17 In your Law it is written that the witness of two
people is true. 18 I am one witness concerning myself, and the Father
who sent me is the other."

19 They asked him, "Where is your Father?"

Jesus answered, "You don't know me and you don't know my Father.
If you knew me, you would also know my Father." 20 He spoke these
words while he was teaching in the temple area known as the treasury.
No one arrested him, because his time hadn't yet come.

21 Jesus continued, "I'm going away. You will look for me, and you will
die in your sin. Where I'm going, you can't come."

22 The Jewish leaders said, "He isn't going to kill himself, is he? Is that
why he said, 'Where I'm going, you can't come'?"

23 He said to them, "You are from below; I'm from above. You are from
this world; I'm not from this world. 24 This is why I told you that you
would die in your sins. If you don't believe that I Am, you will die in
your sins."

25 "Who are you?" they asked.

Jesus replied, "I'm exactly who I have claimed to be from the beginning.
26 I have many things to say in judgment concerning you. The one who
sent me is true, and what I have heard from him I tell the world." 27 They
didn't know he was speaking about his Father. 28 So Jesus said to them,
"When the Human One[y] is lifted up,[z] then you will know that I Am.[a]
Then you will know that I do nothing on my own, but I say just what the
Father has taught me. 29 He who sent me is with me. He doesn't leave
me by myself, because I always do what makes him happy." 30 While
Jesus was saying these things, many people came to believe in him.

Children of Abraham

31 Jesus said to the Jews who believed in him, "You are truly my disciples if you remain faithful to my teaching. 32 Then you will know the
truth, and the truth will set you free."

33 They responded, "We are Abraham's children; we've never been anyone's slaves. How can you say that we will be set free?"

[y] Or *Son of Man* [z] Or *exalted* [a] Or *that I am he*

34Jesus answered, "I assure you that everyone who sins is a slave to
sin. 35A slave isn't a permanent member of the household, but a son is.
36Therefore, if the Son makes you free, you really will be free. 37I know
that you are Abraham's children, yet you want to kill me because you
don't welcome my teaching. 38I'm telling you what I've seen when I am
with the Father, but you are doing what you've heard from your father."

39They replied, "Our father is Abraham."

Jesus responded, "If you were Abraham's children, you would do
Abraham's works. 40Instead, you want to kill me, though I am the one
who has spoken the truth I heard from God. Abraham didn't do this.
41You are doing your father's works."

They said, "Our ancestry isn't in question! The only Father we have
is God!"

42Jesus replied, "If God were your Father, you would love me, for I
came from God. Here I am. I haven't come on my own. God sent me.
43Why don't you understand what I'm saying? It's because you can't
really hear my words. 44Your father is the devil. You are his children,
and you want to do what your father wants. He was a murderer from
the beginning. He has never stood for the truth, because there's no
truth in him. Whenever that liar speaks, he speaks according to his own
nature, because he's a liar and the father of liars. 45Because I speak the
truth, you don't believe me. 46Who among you can show I'm guilty of
sin? Since I speak the truth, why don't you believe me? 47God's children
listen to God's words. You don't listen to me because you aren't God's
children."

48The Jewish opposition answered, "We were right to say that you are
a Samaritan and have a demon, weren't we?"

49"I don't have a demon," Jesus replied. "But I honor my Father and
you dishonor me. 50I'm not trying to bring glory to myself. There's one
who is seeking to glorify me, and he's the judge. 51I assure you that
whoever keeps my word will never die."

Abraham and Jesus

52The Jewish opposition said to Jesus, "Now we know that you have
a demon. Abraham and the prophets died, yet you say, 'Whoever keeps
my word will never die.' 53Are you greater than our father Abraham? He
died and the prophets died, so who do you make yourself out to be?"

54Jesus answered, "If I glorify myself, my glory is meaningless. My
Father, who you say is your God, is the one who glorifies me. 55You don't
know him, but I do. If I said I didn't know him, I would be like you, a
liar. But I do know him, and I keep his word. 56Your father Abraham was
overjoyed that he would see my day. He saw it and was happy."

57“You aren’t even 50 years old!” the Jewish opposition replied. “How
can you say that you have seen Abraham?”

58“I assure you,” Jesus replied, “before Abraham was, I Am.” 59So they
picked up stones to throw at him, but Jesus hid himself and left the
temple.

Jesus heals a blind man

9 As Jesus walked along, he saw a man who was blind from birth.
2Jesus’ disciples asked, “Rabbi, who sinned so that he was born
blind, this man or his parents?”

3Jesus answered, “Neither he nor his parents. This happened so that
God’s mighty works might be displayed in him. 4While it’s daytime,
we must do the works of him who sent me. Night is coming when no
one can work. 5While I am in the world, I am the light of the world.”
6After he said this, he spit on the ground, made mud with the saliva,
and smeared the mud on the man’s eyes. 7Jesus said to him, “Go, wash
in the pool of Siloam” (this word means *sent*). So the man went away
and washed. When he returned, he could see.

Disagreement about the healing

8The man’s neighbors and those who used to see him when he was a
beggar said, “Isn’t this the man who used to sit and beg?”

9Some said, “It is,” and others said, “No, it’s someone who looks
like him.”

But the man said, “Yes, it’s me!”

10So they asked him, “How are you now able to see?”

11He answered, “The man they call Jesus made mud, smeared it on
my eyes, and said, ‘Go to the pool of Siloam and wash.’ So I went and
washed, and then I could see.”

12They asked, “Where is this man?”

He replied, “I don’t know.”

13Then they led the man who had been born blind to the Pharisees.
14Now Jesus made the mud and smeared it on the man’s eyes on a Sabbath day. 15So Pharisees also asked him how he was able to see.

The man told them, “He put mud on my eyes, I washed, and now
I see.”

16Some Pharisees said, “This man isn’t from God, because he breaks
the Sabbath law.” Others said, “How can a sinner do miraculous signs
like these?” So they were divided. 17Some of the Pharisees questioned
the man who had been born blind again: “What do you have to say
about him, since he healed your eyes?”

He replied, “He’s a prophet.”

Conflict over the healing

18 The Jewish leaders didn't believe the man had been blind and received his sight until they called for his parents. 19 The Jewish leaders
asked them, "Is this your son? Are you saying he was born blind? How
can he now see?"

20 His parents answered, "We know he is our son. We know he
was born blind. 21 But we don't know how he now sees, and we don't
know who healed his eyes. Ask him. He's old enough to speak for
himself." 22 His parents said this because they feared the Jewish authorities. This is because the Jewish authorities had already decided
that whoever confessed Jesus to be the Christ would be expelled
from the synagogue. 23 That's why his parents said, "He's old enough.
Ask him."

24 Therefore, they called a second time for the man who had been
born blind and said to him, "Give glory to God. We know this man is a
sinner."

25 The man answered, "I don't know whether he's a sinner. Here's what
I do know: I was blind and now I see."

26 They questioned him: "What did he do to you? How did he heal your
eyes?"

27 He replied, "I already told you, and you didn't listen. Why do you
want to hear it again? Do you want to become his disciples too?"

28 They insulted him: "You are his disciple, but we are Moses' disciples.
29 We know that God spoke to Moses, but we don't know where this
man is from."

30 The man answered, "This is incredible! You don't know where he is
from, yet he healed my eyes! 31 We know that God doesn't listen to sinners. God listens to anyone who is devout and does God's will. 32 No one
has ever heard of a healing of the eyes of someone born blind. 33 If this
man wasn't from God, he couldn't do this."

34 They responded, "You were born completely in sin! How is it that
you dare to teach us?" Then they expelled him.

Jesus finds the man born blind

35 Jesus heard they had expelled the man born blind. Finding him,
Jesus said, "Do you believe in the Human One?"[b]

36 He answered, "Who is he, sir?[c] I want to believe in him."

37 Jesus said, "You have seen him. In fact, he is the one speaking
with you."

38 The man said, "Lord,[d] I believe." And he worshipped Jesus.

[b] Or *Son of Man* [c] Or *Lord* [d] Or *Sir*

Jesus teaches the Pharisees

39 Jesus said, "I have come into the world to exercise judgment so that
those who don't see can see and those who see will become blind."
40 Some Pharisees who were with him heard what he said and asked,
"Surely we aren't blind, are we?"
41 Jesus said to them, "If you were blind, you wouldn't have any sin,
10 but now that you say, 'We see,' your sin remains. 1 I assure you
that whoever doesn't enter into the sheep pen through the gate
but climbs over the wall is a thief and an outlaw. 2 The one who enters
through the gate is the shepherd of the sheep. 3 The guard at the gate
opens the gate for him, and the sheep listen to his voice. He calls his
own sheep by name and leads them out. 4 Whenever he has gathered
all of his sheep, he goes before them and they follow him, because they
know his voice. 5 They won't follow a stranger but will run away because
they don't know the stranger's voice." 6 Those who heard Jesus use this
analogy didn't understand what he was saying.

I am the gate

7 So Jesus spoke again, "I assure you that I am the gate of the sheep.
8 All who came before me were thieves and outlaws, but the sheep didn't
listen to them. 9 I am the gate. Whoever enters through me will be saved.
They will come in and go out and find pasture. 10 The thief enters only to
steal, kill, and destroy. I came so that they could have life—indeed, so
that they could live life to the fullest.

I am the good shepherd

11 "I am the good shepherd. The good shepherd lays down his life for
the sheep. 12 When the hired hand sees the wolf coming, he leaves the
sheep and runs away. That's because he isn't the shepherd; the sheep
aren't really his. So the wolf attacks the sheep and scatters them. 13 He's
only a hired hand and the sheep don't matter to him.
14 "I am the good shepherd. I know my own sheep and they know me,
15 just as the Father knows me and I know the Father. I give up my life
for the sheep. 16 I have other sheep that don't belong to this sheep pen.
I must lead them too. They will listen to my voice and there will be one
flock, with one shepherd.
17 "This is why the Father loves me: I give up my life so that I can take
it up again. 18 No one takes it from me, but I give it up because I want to.
I have the right to give it up, and I have the right to take it up again. I
received this commandment from my Father."
19 There was another division among the Jews because of Jesus'
words. 20 Many of them said, "He has a demon and has lost his mind.

Why listen to him?" [21]Others said, "These aren't the words of someone
who has a demon. Can a demon heal the eyes of people who are blind?"

Jesus at the Festival of Dedication

[22]The time came for the Festival of Dedication[e] in Jerusalem. It was
winter, [23]and Jesus was in the temple, walking in the covered porch
named for Solomon. [24]The Jewish opposition circled around him and
asked, "How long will you test our patience? If you are the Christ, tell
us plainly."

[25]Jesus answered, "I have told you, but you don't believe. The works
I do in my Father's name testify about me, [26]but you don't believe because you don't belong to my sheep. [27]My sheep listen to my voice. I
know them and they follow me. [28]I give them eternal life. They will
never die, and no one will snatch them from my hand. [29]My Father, who
has given them to me, is greater than all, and no one is able to snatch
them from my Father's hand. [30]I and the Father are one."

[31]Again the Jewish opposition picked up stones in order to stone
him. [32]Jesus responded, "I have shown you many good works from the
Father. For which of those works do you stone me?"

[33]The Jewish opposition answered, "We don't stone you for a good
work but for insulting God. You are human, yet you make yourself out
to be God."

[34]Jesus replied, "Isn't it written in your Law, *I have said, you are gods?*[f]
[35]Scripture calls those to whom God's word came *gods*, and scripture
can't be abolished. [36]So how can you say that the one whom the Father
has made holy and sent into the world insults God because he said, 'I
am God's Son'? [37]If I don't do the works of my Father, don't believe me.
[38]But if I do them, and you don't believe me, believe the works so that
you can know and recognize that the Father is in me and I am in the
Father." [39]Again, they wanted to arrest him, but he escaped from them.

Jesus at the Jordan

[40]Jesus went back across the Jordan to the place where John had baptized at first, and he stayed there. [41]Many people came to him. "John
didn't do any miraculous signs," they said, "but everything John said
about this man was true." [42]Many believed in Jesus there.

Lazarus is ill

11 A certain man, Lazarus, was ill. He was from Bethany, the village
of Mary and her sister Martha. ([2]This was the Mary who anointed

[e]Hanukkah [f]Ps 82:6

the Lord with fragrant oil and wiped his feet with her hair. Her brother
Lazarus was ill.) 3So the sisters sent word to Jesus, saying, "Lord, the
one whom you love is ill."

4When he heard this, Jesus said, "This illness isn't fatal. It's for the
glory of God so that God's Son can be glorified through it." 5Jesus loved
Martha, her sister, and Lazarus. 6When he heard that Lazarus was ill,
he stayed where he was. After two days, 7he said to his disciples, "Let's
return to Judea again."

8The disciples replied, "Rabbi, the Jewish opposition wants to stone
you, but you want to go back?"

9Jesus answered, "Aren't there twelve hours in the day? Whoever
walks in the day doesn't stumble because they see the light of the
world. 10But whoever walks in the night does stumble because the light
isn't in them."

11He continued, "Our friend Lazarus is sleeping, but I am going in
order to wake him up."

12The disciples said, "Lord, if he's sleeping, he will get well." 13They
thought Jesus meant that Lazarus was in a deep sleep, but Jesus had
spoken about Lazarus' death.

14Jesus told them plainly, "Lazarus has died. 15For your sakes, I'm glad
I wasn't there so that you can believe. Let's go to him."

16Then Thomas (the one called Didymus) said to the other disciples,
"Let us go too so that we may die with Jesus."

Jesus with Martha and Mary

17When Jesus arrived, he found that Lazarus had already been in the
tomb for four days. 18Bethany was a little less than two miles from Jerusalem. 19Many Jews had come to comfort Martha and Mary after their
brother's death. 20When Martha heard that Jesus was coming, she went
to meet him, while Mary remained in the house. 21Martha said to Jesus,
"Lord, if you had been here, my brother wouldn't have died. 22Even now
I know that whatever you ask God, God will give you."

23Jesus told her, "Your brother will rise again."

24Martha replied, "I know that he will rise in the resurrection on the
last day."

25Jesus said to her, "I am the resurrection and the life. Whoever believes in me will live, even though they die. 26Everyone who lives and
believes in me will never die. Do you believe this?"

27She replied, "Yes, Lord, I believe that you are the Christ, God's Son,
the one who is coming into the world."

28After she said this, she went and spoke privately to her sister Mary,
"The teacher is here and he's calling for you." 29When Mary heard this,

she got up quickly and went to Jesus. 30He hadn't entered the village but was still in the place where Martha had met him. 31When the Jews who were comforting Mary in the house saw her get up quickly and leave, they followed her. They assumed she was going to mourn at the tomb.

32When Mary arrived where Jesus was and saw him, she fell at his feet and said, "Lord, if you had been here, my brother wouldn't have died."

33When Jesus saw her crying and the Jews who had come with her crying also, he was deeply disturbed and troubled. 34He asked, "Where have you laid him?"

They replied, "Lord, come and see."

35Jesus began to cry. 36The Jews said, "See how much he loved him!" 37But some of them said, "He healed the eyes of the man born blind. Couldn't he have kept Lazarus from dying?"

Jesus at Lazarus' tomb

38Jesus was deeply disturbed again when he came to the tomb. It was a cave, and a stone covered the entrance. 39Jesus said, "Remove the stone."

Martha, the sister of the dead man, said, "Lord, the smell will be awful! He's been dead four days."

40Jesus replied, "Didn't I tell you that if you believe, you will see God's glory?" 41So they removed the stone. Jesus looked up and said, "Father, thank you for hearing me. 42I know you always hear me. I say this for the benefit of the crowd standing here so that they will believe that you sent me." 43Having said this, Jesus shouted with a loud voice, "Lazarus, come out!" 44The dead man came out, his feet bound and his hands tied, and his face covered with a cloth. Jesus said to them, "Untie him and let him go."

45Therefore, many of the Jews who came with Mary and saw what Jesus did believed in him. 46But some of them went to the Pharisees and told them what Jesus had done.

Caiaphas prophesies

47Then the chief priests and Pharisees called together the council[g] and said, "What are we going to do? This man is doing many miraculous signs! 48If we let him go on like this, everyone will believe in him. Then the Romans will come and take away both our temple and our people."

49One of them, Caiaphas, who was high priest that year, told them, "You don't know anything! 50You don't see that it is better for you that

[g] Or *Sanhedrin*

one man die for the people rather than the whole nation be destroyed."
51He didn't say this on his own. As high priest that year, he prophesied
that Jesus would soon die for the nation—52and not only for the nation. Jesus would also die so that God's children scattered everywhere
would be gathered together as one. 53From that day on they plotted to
kill him.

The Passover draws near

54Therefore, Jesus was no longer active in public ministry among the
Jewish leaders. Instead, he left Jerusalem and went to a place near the
wilderness, to a city called Ephraim, where he stayed with his disciples.
55It was almost time for the Jewish Passover, and many people went
from the countryside up to Jerusalem to purify themselves through
ritual washing before the Passover. 56They were looking for Jesus. As
they spoke to each other in the temple, they said, "What do you think?
He won't come to the festival, will he?" 57The chief priests and Pharisees
had given orders that anyone who knew where he was should report it,
so they could arrest him.

Chapter Four

The Farewell Discourse

"My Father is glorified when you produce much fruit and in this way prove that you are my disciples. As the Father loved me, I too have loved you. Remain in my love. If you keep my commandments, you will remain in my love, just as I kept my Father's commandments and remain in his love." (John 15:8-10)

4

The Farewell Discourse

In this chapter we turn our attention to what is typically called the Farewell Discourse—the words of Jesus at the Last Supper as he prepared the disciples for his death.

Matthew and Mark tell us very little about what Jesus said and did at the Last Supper, and Luke has just twenty-five verses on the subject. But John's Gospel devotes five *chapters* to it, chapters 13–17. That's 155 verses, almost 25 percent of John's Gospel devoted to the Last Supper, virtually none of which appear in Matthew, Mark, or Luke.

In these five chapters, Jesus tried to prepare the disciples for what was to come. Though they did not understand it, Jesus knew that following the supper, he would go to the garden of Gethsemane and be arrested, then he would be tried, and the next day he would be crucified. As a result, he felt an urgency that night. These would be the last things Jesus would tell his disciples before his death. Imagine how you would feel and what you would say if you were speaking to your children or closest friends, knowing you would be arrested and killed the following day.

I'm reminded of a member of my congregation who, some years ago, was dying of Lou Gehrig's Disease (ALS). He knew that before long he wouldn't be able to speak. He had two little boys. So he set up a tripod with a camcorder on it and began recording, telling his boys the things he wanted them to know as they were growing up. His hope was that the boys would play the tapes when they were in their teen years and then again before they were married. He wanted to teach them the life lessons he would have offered if he had been with them as they grew. In the same way, we can understand the urgency Jesus felt, knowing he had little time left.

In this chapter, we'll consider four things that Jesus taught his disciples on that night as he shared with them his Last Supper.

Blessed If You Do Them

John's account of the Farewell Discourse begins in Chapter 13, with Jesus washing his disciples' feet. In the first century, people wore leather sandals with no socks, walking all day on the dusty roads. Have you ever worn a pair of sandals without socks all day long in the summer? Your feet probably were tired, dirty, and smelled bad by the time you came in for supper. This is why in first-century homes a pitcher of water was often set by the door with a towel and basin. If the household had servants, it would be the job of the lowest servant to wash the feet of the master and guests. If not, the guests washed their own feet.

On a mission trip to Africa several years ago I was rooming with a friend. At the end of the day, we were getting ready for bed and the room had a horrible smell. I finally traced it to my friend's shoes. The smell was truly terrible. He told me they were his favorite shoes, and he'd worn them on mission trips around the world. I said, "Dude, either these shoes stay outside tonight or I do. I can't sleep with them in the room!" He poured some baby powder into the shoes but it didn't help. So he put them outside in the hallway. We could have used a pitcher of water and a basin that night.

There was no servant stationed in the upper room for supper that night as Jesus and his disciples entered. And though there was a pitcher and basin by the door, the disciples had not washed their feet, a fact that seems odd. We can picture them reclining on floor cushions, as was the custom, leaning on an elbow with the food in front of them—thirteen men, at least some of whose feet probably smelled like my friend's shoes.

Why didn't any of the disciples stop to wash their own feet? I've wondered about that. Maybe they were afraid that if they took the pitcher and towel, they might be expected to wash the feet of others. Better to leave the water alone than to have to wash another's feet! I suspect they had been around Jesus long enough to know that serving others might mean washing someone's feet.

In fact, Luke tells us that serving one another was the furthest thing from their minds that night. Here is what he says happened at the Last Supper:

> An argument broke out among the disciples over which one of them should be regarded as the greatest. But Jesus said to them, "The kings of the Gentiles rule over their subjects, and those in authority over them are called 'friends of the people.' But that's not the way it will be with you. Instead, the greatest among you

> must become like a person of lower status and the leader like a servant." (Luke 22:24-26)

Can you imagine? Jesus was going to be crucified the next day, and they were debating which one of them was the greatest. They thought he would be crowned king, and each believed that he deserved to be Jesus' right-hand man.

As we've learned, John's Gospel doesn't show Jesus taking the bread and wine and telling the disciples to "do this in remembrance of me." John has already pointed to the meaning of Communion in the changing of the water to wine and in Jesus' words about the bread of life. In John's Gospel, perhaps in response to the argument reported by Luke, Jesus walked to the door and picked up the pitcher, basin, and towel they had all walked past. Then he got on his knees and, to their shock and embarrassment, Jesus began washing their feet. The disciples were mortified. In fact, Simon Peter initially refused to let Jesus do it. But Jesus said, "Unless I wash you, you won't have a place with me" (13:8b). Then Jesus said to all of them:

> "I have given you an example: Just as I have done, you also must do.... Since you know these things, you will be happy if you do them." (John 13:15, 17)

There's one other thing to know about this passage. You won't pick it up in English, but the original Greek says that before washing their feet, Jesus laid his robe down. The word used is the same one used when Jesus described what would happen on the cross: he would lay down his life. Then, when he finished washing their feet, he took up his robe again, much as after the cross he would take up his life again. When he washed the disciples' feet in the upper room, Jesus was prefiguring his crucifixion and resurrection.

Jesus told his disciples that blessings—the Greek word is *makarios*, which means happiness or a sense of well-being—come from serving others, not from being served. In the act of washing their feet, Jesus had shown the disciples what it means to be one of his followers. Being a servant of others is a fundamental principle of the Christian faith. Jesus was saying that if we play the role of servant, we will find happiness and the fulfillment we typically seek in so many other ways.

I once interviewed the head of the psychology department at a Kansas City university. We spoke about contemporary insights in the field of psychology and their connection with Christian spirituality. She noted that the field of positive psychology has found that for many people who struggle with depression, serving others can be one of the most effective forms of therapy. She said, "So many of the things researchers in my field are discovering are the things I learned as a child in Sunday school." Researchers have learned the same thing Jesus taught: we are made to serve.

Both liberals and conservatives in the Catholic Church admire Pope Francis's humility and concern for the poor. When he was Cardinal Jorge Bergoglio in Buenos Aires, he cooked for himself, and often he refused a limousine and instead rode public transportation. What stands out to me about that time in his life, though, was a report from a poor village near Buenos Aires where many others would not go because they considered it too dangerous.

According to the report, a church in that village, like many Catholic churches, was planning to remember Jesus' foot washing during a service commemorating the Last Supper, in which the priest would wash the feet of ordinary church members. Cardinal Bergoglio came to mass at the village that day and met twenty-seven-year-old Cristian Marcelo Reynoso, a garbage collector. Here is what Marcelo said about the experience: "I was at my worst and I needed help.

When the Mass started, [the cardinal] knelt down and washed my feet. It hit me hard. It was such a beautiful experience."[1] The cardinal washed the feet of AIDS patients, drug addicts, and the poor as he sought to demonstrate the love of Christ.

Jesus wanted to make sure his disciples got it. The story in John 13 encourages us to ask this question: Are you—am I—worried about who appears to be the greatest, or are we focused on humbly serving others?

IN MY FATHER'S HOUSE...

At the Last Supper Jesus spoke about trust, just after he told his disciples he would be leaving them. He predicted that Peter would deny him three times. Then he sought to reassure them, saying,

> "Don't be troubled. Trust in God. Trust also in me. My Father's house has room to spare. If that weren't the case, would I have told you that I'm going to prepare a place for you? When I go to prepare a place for you, I will return and take you to be with me so that where I am you will be too. You know the way to the place I'm going." (John 14:1-4)

We often share this passage at the death of a loved one. The words of reassurance that Jesus spoke to his disciples at the Last Supper in the face of his imminent death also speak to us when we lose a loved one. A literal translation of the original Greek has Jesus saying, "Don't let your hearts be shaken up." Then he called the disciples to trust in God and trust in him.

The Greek word for *trust* used by John in 14:1-4 means, at its core, to be persuaded about the truth of something, to have conviction that then leads to action. In John's account of the Last Supper, Jesus called for his followers to hold a deep conviction that he was all that he had declared in the "I AM" sayings. There is something about trusting in Jesus that makes it possible for our hearts not to be "shaken up" when we're walking through terrible times. Of course, we will experience pain and loss. But we will regain our bearings when we trust in Christ.

There is something about trusting in Jesus that makes it possible for our hearts not to be "shaken up" when we're walking through terrible times.

I ask you a simple question: What do you trust in? When you strip away everything else, what is it—at the bedrock in your life—that you trust in? Some people trust in their abilities. Some trust in wealth. Some trust in the military. Some trust in their own intellect. But Christ calls us to trust in him, to count on him.

Mike, a young man in our congregation, had two small children. One terrible night, Mike died in his sleep. Ingrid, his wife, said to me at church after the funeral service, "It is the things I've learned here that I'm trusting in now—that the worst thing is never the last thing and that God will not abandon us. I am trusting that Mike is with him. That's what makes his loss bearable today."

After asking the disciples to trust in him, Jesus said, "My Father's house has room to spare" (John 14:2). The old King James Version translated it this way: "In my Father's house are many mansions." But if we look at the original Greek, Jesus seems to be saying something slightly different: "In my Father's household there are many rooms." The Greek word for the Father's "household" is *oikos*, which was the basic unit of society in ancient times: the family. And the family—which included grandparents, adult children, grandchildren, and siblings—shared a home. In the first-century Jewish world, as is still true among many Palestinians and Jews today, when a son or daughter married, a room simply was added onto the house. New and old members shared responsibility, they shared life together, they were family. That was *oikos*.

Jesus said that by trusting in him we become a part of God's household, and heaven is our Father's house, where there are plenty of rooms.

Several years ago, I became hooked on the television program, *Downton Abbey*, set in the early 1900s in England. Downton Abbey is actually the name of the home where the Crawley family lives. The program was filmed at a real castle in England, Highclere Castle, and the stories were about the various members of the household who live in it. As I read this passage about our Father's house and the many rooms there, I think of that castle. There is a home big enough for everyone.

But, more than Downton Abbey, when I consider Jesus' words I think of my own children, now grown. One Friday night, my wife was out of town and I had supper at the home of our daughter and son-in-law, Danielle and JT. As I was leaving, I noticed one of the pictures on their living room wall. It showed the house where LaVon and I live, the house where my children grew up, and beneath it was a caption: *Home*. Our Father's house is home. We will be with him and with those whom we've loved, members of his household.

THE PROMISE OF THE COMFORTER

Jesus continued his Farewell Discourse with the promise of the Holy Spirit, which would become a prominent theme in these chapters.

> "I will ask the Father, and he will send another Companion, who will be with you forever. This Companion is the Spirit of Truth, whom the world can't receive because it neither sees him nor recognizes him. You know him, because he lives with you and will be with you." (John 14:16-17)

Repeatedly in these chapters, Jesus promised that after his death, God would send the Holy Spirit. The Greek word for Spirit is *pneuma*, a word that literally means "breath" or "wind" or "air." You will recognize it in our word *pneumonia*, or better, *pneumatic*, which is when you power things by compressed air. There is power in wind and breath. In the Old Testament, God scooped up the dust of the earth and breathed *pneuma* into the first creatures, Adam and Eve. They had life once God breathed into them the spirit, the *pneuma*, or in Hebrew the *ruach.*

John alone records Jesus calling the Holy Spirit the *paraclete. Paraclete* can be translated as advocate, counselor, comforter, helper, or encourager and means someone who comes alongside you. It was a term used for an advocate or defense attorney in courtroom trials—someone who was on your side, helping, advocating for you. So the Holy Spirit would come alongside us and be our advocate.

It's fascinating to see that at the end of the Gospel of John, Jesus breathed on his disciples just as God breathed on Adam and Eve. He said to the disciples, "Receive the Holy Spirit" (John 20:22), and with that they received the Spirit, God's breath.

The point, for the disciples and for us, is that Jesus did not leave us alone. He promised that God, by his Spirit, would continue to be at work in his followers. Through the Spirit we experience God's indwelling presence. It is the Spirit that draws us to Christ, that changes us as we put our trust in Christ, that nudges us in the right direction when we're paying attention, and that comforts us when we feel God's presence holding and keeping us.

With some regularity I experience both God's comfort from the Spirit, but also the leadership and guidance of the Spirit. One day not long ago I felt an urging to go visit one of our church members at the hospital. She wasn't on my schedule for the day. I had very little time, and the hospital was a twenty-five-minute drive from my office. But I've learned to pay attention to these nudges. I arrived at the hospital and visited the woman, shared Scripture, and prayed. It was a meaningful visit, and I offered encouragement and care for the woman and her husband. I was leaving to return to my office when the phone rang, and I learned there was someone else in the hospital whom I might visit; otherwise another of our pastors would go the next day. I looked at my watch, realized I was running late for an appointment, and started to text my reply that I'd run out of time.

But as I walked to the car I felt another nudge: "Push back your other appointment; I need you to see this person." I went back into the hospital to visit the additional patient. As I entered his room I found that the man was near death. His children were there with him. They were so surprised and grateful to see me. I shared a Scripture, anointed their father with oil, and prayed with them, committing his life to God. Not long after that he passed away. His daughter felt that God had sent me. I also felt that God had sent me. But I almost missed it. Some speak of these as coincidences. I see them as "God-incidents."

I try to listen to the whisper of the Spirit. When I'm paying attention, I often find myself in the midst of meaningful situations where God is at work.

Are you paying attention to the Spirit? Are you open and inviting the Spirit to work through you? Are you watching for the Spirit to work through others? Jesus promised his disciples that, after his death, he would send the Spirit who would continue to guide, encourage, and comfort them.

THE VINE AND THE BRANCHES

In the previous chapter we discussed the "I AM" sayings of Jesus. The last of those sayings was part of the Final Discourse:

> "I am the true vine, and my Father is the vineyard keeper. He removes any of my branches that don't produce fruit, and he trims any branch that produces fruit so that it will produce even more fruit. You are already trimmed because of the word I have spoken to you. Remain in me, and I will remain in you. A branch can't produce fruit by itself, but must remain in the vine. Likewise, you can't produce fruit unless you remain in me. I am the vine; you are the branches. If you remain in me and I in you, then you will produce much fruit. Without me, you can't do anything." (John 15:1-5)

I'm not much of a wine drinker, but I've enjoyed learning about raising grapes and the process of producing wine. I've been on tours of wineries in South Africa, Italy, and Napa Valley in California. I love the idea that in the Old Testament, God was the vineyard keeper and Israel was the vineyard or vine. God tended her and pruned her and prepared her so that she might bear fruit.

Jesus changed the metaphor. He said that he is the vine and his followers are the branches. We know that no branch can bear fruit by itself; it must stay firmly attached to the vine. Science tells us that the roots supply the plant with water and nitrogen and other nutrients. The leaves take in carbon dioxide and light, producing sugars, which are transformed into the fruit. Imagine what would happen if we were to cut a branch from a vine; it would stand no chance of producing fruit.

Jesus was saying, "If you are to be fruitful, you must remain connected to me." How do we remain connected to Christ? We talk with him. We worship. We pray. We read Scripture. We do his work.

And we invite the Spirit to remain in us. We meet with others to study and encourage one another. As the Spirit remains in us, we remain in Christ.

In the Synoptic Gospels, Jesus told the disciples to remember him when they broke bread and drank wine. Bread and wine were a part of nearly every meal, so originally Jesus may not have intended a special Eucharistic meal, or Holy Communion; he may have meant that whenever we break bread we should remember him and remain with him. That's one reason why we always pause and offer a prayer before we eat, recognizing at each meal that Christ is with us.

One of the great prayers of the Christian faith is the Prayer of St. Patrick, in which the author invites Christ to remain close by.

> Christ with me, Christ before me, Christ behind me,
> Christ in me, Christ beneath me, Christ above me,
> Christ on my right, Christ on my left,
> Christ when I lie down, Christ when I sit down,
> Christ in the heart of everyone who thinks of me,
> Christ in the mouth of everyone who speaks of me,
> Christ in the eye that sees me,
> Christ in the ear that hears me.[2]

That is the prayer of someone who remained connected to the vine! So I'd ask you, are you remaining in Christ? Are you daily walking with him, mindful of him, talking with him, drawing strength from him, reflecting him to others? The Holy Spirit is the power of God and the presence of God at work in your life, and anytime you experience God, anytime God does something in your life, it's the work of the Holy Spirit.

CHRIST'S COMMANDMENT: LOVE ONE ANOTHER

Vines, if tended properly, will bear fruit. And if we are branches connected to the vine, so will we. This is what Jesus was calling us to—fruitfulness, as we read in John 15:

> "My Father is glorified when you produce much fruit and in this way prove that you are my disciples. As the Father loved me, I too have loved you. Remain in my love. If you keep my commandments, you will remain in my love, just as I kept my Father's commandments and remain in his love. . . . You didn't choose me, but I chose you and appointed you so that you could go and produce fruit and so that your fruit could last. As a result, whatever you ask the Father in my name, he will give you."
>
> (John 15:8-10, 16)

What is the fruit we are meant to bear? Over and over again in his Final Discourse, Jesus said that we bear fruit by keeping his commandments. It's what he requires of his disciples. If we do what Jesus tells us to, we are bearing fruit.

If that's true, then what are the commandments? Undoubtedly there are many, but they all seem to come down to one thing. "This is my commandment: love each other just as I have loved you. No one has greater love than to give up one's life for one's friends" (15:12-13).

What does it look like to be a mature Christian? In some churches it's how much of the Bible you memorize. In some churches it's how orthodox your theology is. In some churches it's how many mission trips you have taken. But Jesus simplified it: the measure of spiritual maturity is love.

Seen in this light, the whole of Christian ethics comes down to one question: What is the most loving thing to do? We should ask it in every situation. The answer is not always clear, but Jesus gave us guidance, which takes us right back to the washing of feet. Jesus taught us and showed us that to love is to serve, to bless, to give life, to want the best for the other.

Paul wrote that love is the more excellent way. Jesus said the entire Old Testament comes down to loving God and loving neighbor. James called love the "royal law" (James 2:8). I love that moment in the musical *Les Miserables* when Fontine, Valjean, and Éponine all sing together, "To love another person is to see the face of God."

Love is the essential fruit of our faith. It doesn't matter how much you know, how correct your theology is, how much money you give; if you don't practice love, you've missed the mark. You are a vine branch that is unfruitful, the kind that Jesus said needs to be pruned and cast into the fire!

Love is the essential fruit of our faith. It doesn't matter how much you know, how correct your theology is, how much money you give; if you don't practice love, you've missed the mark.

Love is what heals the world and gives life. In marriage, when both partners see themselves as seeking to serve, bless, and build up the other, the marriage will be healthy and beautiful. Whenever you're trying to decide the right thing to do, you will never go wrong by asking, "What is the most loving thing I can do?"

Love is found in small things and sometimes in big things. It is not a feeling, but a way of acting. It is meant, as we mature in Christ, to become second nature. It shows itself in a thousand ways—sharing meals and cards at the loss of a loved one, taking off work to be with a family during surgery, supporting others when they are down. It is mowing another's yard, taking care of a neighbor's dog when an emergency calls her out of town. It is leaving an extra tip for the person who cleans your room at the hotel. Love is meant to be the rhythm of our lives. It's our daily mission.

Wesley Autrey knew love, and he lived it. One day a stranger, Cameron Hollopeter, had a seizure in the subway and fell onto the tracks. Without hesitating, Autrey jumped down to help as a train approached. He held Hollopeter in the drainage trench between the tracks as the train roared by overhead, just inches away from their bodies. Autrey became known as the Subway Samaritan, the Hero of Harlem. *Time Magazine* recognized him as one of the 100 most influential people in the world. Autrey later told the *New York Times*, "I don't feel like I did something spectacular; I just saw someone who needed help. I did what I felt was right."[3]

When I heard Autrey's story, I was reminded of Jesus' words as he finished describing the vine and the branches: "Greater love has no one than this: to lay down one's life for one's friends" (John 15:13 NIV). Hollopeter wasn't even Autrey's friend, but he was a neighbor.

You will probably never be asked to jump in front of a subway train. But every day you're asked by God to bless, to selflessly serve, to show love in tangible ways. You're asked to love your spouse and demonstrate that love, even when your spouse is being irritating. You're asked to meet the needs of people you work with, even when they aren't nice. You're asked to serve your community, even if you're nervous because you've never been in that neighborhood at night. In our congregation we ask each member to take vacation time at least once every five years to go on a mission trip.

Answer the call to serve. Invite the Holy Spirit to lead, guide, and empower you. Remain in Christ, and obey his command to love. In the Farewell Discourse, these were Jesus' final words to the disciples—and to us.

Dear Lord, help me have a heart to serve others rather than seeking to be served. Give me the humble job, the one no one else wants. Help me to listen for the leading of your Spirit. May I abide in you, Lord, constantly connected, that I might bear the fruit of your love. In your holy name. Amen.

The Gospel of John: Part Four

John 12–17 (CEB)

John 12 recounts the events of the last week of Jesus' life. John chapters 13–17 captures the events and Jesus' discourse at the Last Supper

John 11:51
one man die for the people rather than the whole nation be destroyed."
[51]He didn't say this on his own. As high priest that year, he prophesied
that Jesus would soon die for the nation—[52]and not only for the nation. Jesus would also die so that God's children scattered everywhere
would be gathered together as one. [53]From that day on they plotted to
kill him.

The Passover draws near

[54]Therefore, Jesus was no longer active in public ministry among the
Jewish leaders. Instead, he left Jerusalem and went to a place near the
wilderness, to a city called Ephraim, where he stayed with his disciples.
[55]It was almost time for the Jewish Passover, and many people went
ide up to Jerusalem to purify themselves through
re the Passover. [56]They were looking for Jesus. As
other in the temple, they said, "What do you think?
e festival, will he?" [57]The chief priests and Pharisees
at anyone who knew where he was should report it,
est him.

START
THIS WEEK'S
READING AT
CHAPTER 12

Mary anoints Jesus' feet

12 Six days before Passover, Jesus came to Bethany, home of Lazarus, whom Jesus had raised from the dead. [2]Lazarus and his sisters hosted a dinner for him. Martha served and Lazarus was among
those who joined him at the table. [3]Then Mary took an extraordinary
amount, almost three-quarters of a pound,[h] of very expensive perfume
made of pure nard. She anointed Jesus' feet with it, then wiped his
feet dry with her hair. The house was filled with the aroma of the perfume. [4]Judas Iscariot, one of his disciples (the one who was about to
betray him), complained, [5]"This perfume was worth a year's wages![i]
Why wasn't it sold and the money given to the poor?" ([6]He said this not
because he cared about the poor but because he was a thief. He carried
the money bag and would take what was in it.)
[7]Then Jesus said, "Leave her alone. This perfume was to be used in
preparation for my burial, and this is how she has used it. [8]You will
always have the poor among you, but you won't always have me."
[9]Many Jews learned that he was there. They came not only because
of Jesus but also to see Lazarus, whom he had raised from the dead.
[10]The chief priests decided that they would kill Lazarus too. [11]It was because of Lazarus that many of the Jews had deserted them and come to
believe in Jesus.

[h]Or *a litra*, a Roman pound, approximately twelve ounces [i]Or *three hundred denaria*

Jesus enters Jerusalem

12 The next day the great crowd that had come for the festival heard
that Jesus was coming to Jerusalem. 13 They took palm branches and
went out to meet him. They shouted,

"Hosanna!
Blessings on the one who comes in the name of the Lord![j]
Blessings on the king of Israel!"

14 Jesus found a young donkey and sat on it, just as it is written,

15 *Don't be afraid, Daughter Zion.*
Look! Your king is coming,
sitting on a donkey's colt.[k]

16 His disciples didn't understand these things at first. After he was
glorified, they remembered that these things had been written about
him and that they had done these things to him.

17 The crowd who had been with him when he called Lazarus out of the
tomb and raised him from the dead were testifying about him. 18 That's
why the crowd came to meet him, because they had heard about this
miraculous sign that he had done. 19 Therefore, the Pharisees said to
each other, "See! You've accomplished nothing! Look! The whole world
is following him!"

Jesus teaches about his death

20 Some Greeks were among those who had come up to worship at the
festival. 21 They came to Philip, who was from Bethsaida in Galilee, and
made a request: "Sir, we want to see Jesus." 22 Philip told Andrew, and
Andrew and Philip told Jesus.

23 Jesus replied, "The time has come for the Human One[l] to be glorified. 24 I assure you that unless a grain of wheat falls into the earth
and dies, it can only be a single seed. But if it dies, it bears much fruit.
25 Those who love their lives will lose them, and those who hate their
lives in this world will keep them forever. 26 Whoever serves me must
follow me. Wherever I am, there my servant will also be. My Father will
honor whoever serves me.

27 "Now *I am deeply troubled.*[m] What should I say? 'Father, save me
from this time'? No, for this is the reason I have come to this time.
28 Father, glorify your name!"

Then a voice came from heaven, "I have glorified it, and I will glorify
it again."

29 The crowd standing there heard and said, "It's thunder." Others
said, "An angel spoke to him."

[j] Ps 118:26 [k] Zech 9:9 [l] Or *Son of Man* [m] Ps 6:2

John 12:30

30 Jesus replied, "This voice wasn't for my benefit but for yours. 31 Now is the time for judgment of this world. Now this world's ruler will be thrown out. 32 When I am lifted up[n] from the earth, I will draw everyone to me." (33 He said this to show how he was going to die.)

34 The crowd responded, "We have heard from the Law that the Christ remains forever. How can you say that the Human One[o] must be lifted up? Who is this Human One?"[p]

35 Jesus replied, "The light is with you for only a little while. Walk while you have the light so that darkness doesn't overtake you. Those who walk in the darkness don't know where they are going. 36 As long as you have the light, believe in the light so that you might become people whose lives are determined by the light." After Jesus said these things, he went away and hid from them.

Fulfillment of prophecy

37 Jesus had done many miraculous signs before the people, but they didn't believe in him. 38 This was to fulfill the word of the prophet Isaiah:

Lord, who has believed through our message?
To whom is the arm of the Lord fully revealed?[q]

39 Isaiah explains why they couldn't believe:

40 *He made their eyes blind*
and closed their minds
so that they might not see with their eyes,
understand with their minds,
and turn their lives around—
and I would heal them.[r]

41 Isaiah said these things because he saw Jesus' glory; he spoke about Jesus. 42 Even so, many leaders believed in him, but they wouldn't acknowledge their faith because they feared that the Pharisees would expel them from the synagogue. 43 They believed, but they loved human praise more than God's glory.

Summary of Jesus' teaching

44 Jesus shouted, "Whoever believes in me doesn't believe in me but in the one who sent me. 45 Whoever sees me sees the one who sent me. 46 I have come as a light into the world so that everyone who believes in me won't live in darkness. 47 If people hear my words and don't keep them, I don't judge them. I didn't come to judge the world but to save it. 48 Whoever rejects me and doesn't receive my words will be judged at the last day by the word I have spoken. 49 I don't speak on my own,

[n]Or *exalted* [o]Or *Son of Man* [p]Or *Son of Man* [q]Isa 53:1 [r]Isa 6:10

but the Father who sent me commanded me regarding what I should
speak and say. 50 I know that his commandment is eternal life. Therefore, whatever I say is just as the Father has said to me."

Foot washing

13 Before the Festival of Passover, Jesus knew that his time had
come to leave this world and go to the Father. Having loved his
own who were in the world, he loved them fully.

2 Jesus and his disciples were sharing the evening meal. The devil had
already provoked Judas, Simon Iscariot's son, to betray Jesus. 3 Jesus
knew the Father had given everything into his hands and that he had
come from God and was returning to God. 4 So he got up from the table
and took off his robes. Picking up a linen towel, he tied it around his
waist. 5 Then he poured water into a washbasin and began to wash the
disciples' feet, drying them with the towel he was wearing. 6 When
Jesus came to Simon Peter, Peter said to him, "Lord, are you going to
wash my feet?"

7 Jesus replied, "You don't understand what I'm doing now, but you
will understand later."

8 "No!" Peter said. "You will never wash my feet!"

Jesus replied, "Unless I wash you, you won't have a place with me."

9 Simon Peter said, "Lord, not only my feet but also my hands and my
head!"

10 Jesus responded, "Those who have bathed need only to have their
feet washed, because they are completely clean. You disciples are clean,
but not every one of you." 11 He knew who would betray him. That's why
he said, "Not every one of you is clean."

12 After he washed the disciples' feet, he put on his robes and returned
to his place at the table. He said to them, "Do you know what I've done
for you? 13 You call me 'Teacher' and 'Lord,' and you speak correctly, because I am. 14 If I, your Lord and teacher, have washed your feet, you too
must wash each other's feet. 15 I have given you an example: Just as I
have done, you also must do. 16 I assure you, servants aren't greater than
their master, nor are those who are sent greater than the one who sent
them. 17 Since you know these things, you will be happy if you do them.
18 I'm not speaking about all of you. I know those whom I've chosen.
But this is to fulfill the scripture, *The one who eats my bread has turned
against me.*[s]

19 "I'm telling you this now, before it happens, so that when it does
happen you will believe that I Am. 20 I assure you that whoever receives

[s] Ps 41:9

someone I send receives me, and whoever receives me receives the one
who sent me."

Announcement of the betrayal

21After he said these things, Jesus was deeply disturbed and testified,
"I assure you, one of you will betray me."

22His disciples looked at each other, confused about which of them
he was talking about. 23One of the disciples, the one whom Jesus loved,
was at Jesus' side. 24Simon Peter nodded at him to get him to ask Jesus
who he was talking about. 25Leaning back toward Jesus, this disciple
asked, "Lord, who is it?"

26Jesus answered, "It's the one to whom I will give this piece of
bread once I have dipped into the bowl." Then he dipped the piece of
bread and gave it to Judas, Simon Iscariot's son. 27After Judas took
the bread, Satan entered into him. Jesus told him, "What you are about
to do, do quickly." 28No one sitting at the table understood why Jesus
said this to him. 29Some thought that, since Judas kept the money bag,
Jesus told him, "Go, buy what we need for the feast," or that he should
give something to the poor. 30So when Judas took the bread, he left
immediately. And it was night.

Love commandment

31When Judas was gone, Jesus said, "Now the Human One[t] has been
glorified, and God has been glorified in him. 32If God has been glorified
in him, God will also glorify the Human One[u] in himself and will glorify
him immediately. 33Little children, I'm with you for a little while longer.
You will look for me—but, just as I told the Jewish leaders, I also tell
you now—'Where I'm going, you can't come.'

34"I give you a new commandment: Love each other. Just as I have
loved you, so you also must love each other. 35This is how everyone will
know that you are my disciples, when you love each other."

Announcement of Peter's denial

36Simon Peter said to Jesus, "Lord, where are you going?"

Jesus answered, "Where I am going, you can't follow me now, but you
will follow later."

37Peter asked, "Lord, why can't I follow you now? I'll give up my life
for you."

38Jesus replied, "Will you give up your life for me? I assure you that
you will deny me three times before the rooster crows.

[t]Or *Son of Man* [u]Or *Son of Man*

The way, the truth, and the life

14 "Don't be troubled. Trust in God. Trust also in me. 2My Father's
house has room to spare. If that weren't the case, would I have
told you that I'm going to prepare a place for you? 3When I go to prepare
a place for you, I will return and take you to be with me so that where I
am you will be too. 4You know the way to the place I'm going."
5Thomas asked, "Lord, we don't know where you are going. How can
we know the way?"
6Jesus answered, "I am the way, the truth, and the life. No one comes
to the Father except through me. 7If you have really known me, you will
also know the Father. From now on you know him and have seen him."
8Philip said, "Lord, show us the Father; that will be enough for us."
9Jesus replied, "Don't you know me, Philip, even after I have been
with you all this time? Whoever has seen me has seen the Father. How
can you say, 'Show us the Father'? 10Don't you believe that I am in the
Father and the Father is in me? The words I have spoken to you I don't
speak on my own. The Father who dwells in me does his works. 11Trust
me when I say that I am in the Father and the Father is in me, or at least
believe on account of the works themselves. 12I assure you that whoever
believes in me will do the works that I do. They will do even greater
works than these because I am going to the Father. 13I will do whatever
you ask for in my name, so that the Father can be glorified in the Son.
14When you ask me for anything in my name, I will do it.

I won't leave you as orphans

15"If you love me, you will keep my commandments. 16I will ask the
Father, and he will send another Companion,[v] who will be with you forever. 17This Companion is the Spirit of Truth, whom the world can't
receive because it neither sees him nor recognizes him. You know him,
because he lives with you and will be with you.
18"I won't leave you as orphans. I will come to you. 19Soon the world
will no longer see me, but you will see me. Because I live, you will live
too. 20On that day you will know that I am in my Father, you are in me,
and I am in you. 21Whoever has my commandments and keeps them
loves me. Whoever loves me will be loved by my Father, and I will love
them and reveal myself to them."
22Judas (not Judas Iscariot) asked, "Lord, why are you about to reveal
yourself to us and not to the world?"
23Jesus answered, "Whoever loves me will keep my word. My Father
will love them, and we will come to them and make our home with

[v] Or *Advocate*

them. 24Whoever doesn't love me doesn't keep my words. The word that you hear isn't mine. It is the word of the Father who sent me.

25"I have spoken these things to you while I am with you. 26The Companion,[w] the Holy Spirit, whom the Father will send in my name, will teach you everything and will remind you of everything I told you.

27"Peace I leave with you. My peace I give you. I give to you not as the world gives. Don't be troubled or afraid. 28You have heard me tell you, 'I'm going away and returning to you.' If you loved me, you would be happy that I am going to the Father, because the Father is greater than me. 29I have told you before it happens so that when it happens you will believe. 30I won't say much more to you because this world's ruler is coming. He has nothing on me. 31Rather, he comes so that the world will know that I love the Father and do just as the Father has commanded me. Get up. We're leaving this place.

I am the true vine

15 "I am the true vine, and my Father is the vineyard keeper. 2He removes any of my branches that don't produce fruit, and he trims any branch that produces fruit so that it will produce even more fruit. 3You are already trimmed because of the word I have spoken to you. 4Remain in me, and I will remain in you. A branch can't produce fruit by itself, but must remain in the vine. Likewise, you can't produce fruit unless you remain in me. 5I am the vine; you are the branches. If you remain in me and I in you, then you will produce much fruit. Without me, you can't do anything. 6If you don't remain in me, you will be like a branch that is thrown out and dries up. Those branches are gathered up, thrown into a fire, and burned. 7If you remain in me and my words remain in you, ask for whatever you want and it will be done for you. 8My Father is glorified when you produce much fruit and in this way prove that you are my disciples.

Love each other

9"As the Father loved me, I too have loved you. Remain in my love. 10If you keep my commandments, you will remain in my love, just as I kept my Father's commandments and remain in his love. 11I have said these things to you so that my joy will be in you and your joy will be complete. 12This is my commandment: love each other just as I have loved you. 13No one has greater love than to give up one's life for one's friends. 14You are my friends if you do what I command you. 15I don't call you servants any longer, because servants don't know what their master is

[w]Or *Advocate*

doing. Instead, I call you friends, because everything I heard from my
Father I have made known to you. 16You didn't choose me, but I chose
you and appointed you so that you could go and produce fruit and so
that your fruit could last. As a result, whatever you ask the Father in my
name, he will give you. 17I give you these commandments so that you
can love each other.

If the world hates you

18"If the world hates you, know that it hated me first. 19If you belonged to the world, the world would love you as its own. However, I
have chosen you out of the world, and you don't belong to the world.
This is why the world hates you. 20Remember what I told you, 'Servants
aren't greater than their master.' If the world harassed me, it will harass
you too. If it kept my word, it will also keep yours. 21The world will do
all these things to you on account of my name, because it doesn't know
the one who sent me.

22"If I hadn't come and spoken to the people of this world, they
wouldn't be sinners. But now they have no excuse for their sin. 23Who-
ever hates me also hates the Father. 24If I hadn't done works among
them that no one else had done, they wouldn't be sinners. But now they
have seen and hated both me and my Father. 25This fulfills the word
written in their Law, *They hated me without a reason.*[x]

26"When the Companion[y] comes, whom I will send from the Father—
the Spirit of Truth who proceeds from the Father—he will testify about
me. 27You will testify too, because you have been with me from the
16 beginning. 1I have said these things to you so that you won't fall
away. 2They will expel you from the synagogue. The time is coming when those who kill you will think that they are doing a service to
God. 3They will do these things because they don't know the Father or
me. 4But I have said these things to you so that when their time comes,
you will remember that I told you about them.

I go away

"I didn't say these things to you from the beginning, because I was
with you. 5But now I go away to the one who sent me. None of you ask
me, 'Where are you going?' 6Yet because I have said these things to you,
you are filled with sorrow. 7I assure you that it is better for you that I go
away. If I don't go away, the Companion[z] won't come to you. But if I go,
I will send him to you. 8When he comes, he will show the world it was
wrong about sin, righteousness, and judgment. 9He will show the world

[x]Pss 35:19; 69:4 [y]Or *Advocate* [z]Or *Advocate*

it was wrong about sin because they don't believe in me. 10He will show the world it was wrong about righteousness because I'm going to the Father and you won't see me anymore. 11He will show the world it was wrong about judgment because this world's ruler stands condemned.

I still have many things to say

12"I have much more to say to you, but you can't handle it now. 13However, when the Spirit of Truth comes, he will guide you in all truth. He won't speak on his own, but will say whatever he hears and will proclaim to you what is to come. 14He will glorify me, because he will take what is mine and proclaim it to you. 15Everything that the Father has is mine. That's why I said that the Spirit takes what is mine and will proclaim it to you. 16Soon you won't be able to see me; soon after that, you will see me."

I will see you again

17Some of Jesus' disciples said to each other, "What does he mean: 'Soon you won't see me, and soon after that you will see me' and 'Because I'm going to the Father'? 18What does he mean by 'soon'? We don't understand what he's talking about."

19Jesus knew they wanted to ask him, so he said, "Are you trying to find out from each other what I meant when I said, 'Soon you won't see me, and soon after that you will see me'? 20I assure you that you will cry and lament, and the world will be happy. You will be sorrowful, but your sorrow will turn into joy. 21When a woman gives birth, she has pain because her time has come. But when the child is born, she no longer remembers her distress because of her joy that a child has been born into the world. 22In the same way, you have sorrow now; but I will see you again, and you will be overjoyed. No one takes away your joy. 23In that day, you won't ask me anything. I assure you that the Father will give you whatever you ask in my name. 24Up to now, you have asked nothing in my name. Ask and you will receive so that your joy will be complete.

I have conquered the world

25"I've been using figures of speech with you. The time is coming when I will no longer speak to you in such analogies. Instead, I will tell you plainly about the Father. 26In that day you will ask in my name. I'm not saying that I will ask the Father on your behalf. 27The Father himself loves you, because you have loved me and believed that I came from God. 28I left the Father and came into the world. I tell you again: I am leaving the world and returning to the Father."

29His disciples said, "See! Now you speak plainly; you aren't using figures of speech. 30Now we know that you know everything and you don't need anyone to ask you. Because of this we believe you have come from God."

31Jesus replied, "Now you believe? 32Look! A time is coming—and is here!—when each of you will be scattered to your own homes and you will leave me alone. I'm not really alone, for the Father is with me. 33I've said these things to you so that you will have peace in me. In the world you have distress. But be encouraged! I have conquered the world."

Jesus prays

17 When Jesus finished saying these things, he looked up to heaven and said, "Father, the time has come. Glorify your Son, so that the Son can glorify you. 2You gave him authority over everyone so that he could give eternal life to everyone you gave him. 3This is eternal life: to know you, the only true God, and Jesus Christ whom you sent. 4I have glorified you on earth by finishing the work you gave me to do. 5Now, Father, glorify me in your presence with the glory I shared with you before the world was created.

6"I have revealed your name to the people you gave me from this world. They were yours and you gave them to me, and they have kept your word. 7Now they know that everything you have given me comes from you. 8This is because I gave them the words that you gave me, and they received them. They truly understood that I came from you, and they believed that you sent me.

9"I'm praying for them. I'm not praying for the world but for those you gave me, because they are yours. 10Everything that is mine is yours and everything that is yours is mine; I have been glorified in them. 11I'm no longer in the world, but they are in the world, even as I'm coming to you. Holy Father, watch over them in your name, the name you gave me, that they will be one just as we are one. 12When I was with them, I watched over them in your name, the name you gave to me, and I kept them safe. None of them were lost, except the one who was destined for destruction, so that scripture would be fulfilled. 13Now I'm coming to you and I say these things while I'm in the world so that they can share completely in my joy. 14I gave your word to them and the world hated them, because they don't belong to this world, just as I don't belong to this world. 15I'm not asking that you take them out of this world but that you keep them safe from the evil one. 16They don't belong to this world, just as I don't belong to this world. 17Make them holy in the truth; your word is truth. 18As you sent me into the world, so I have sent them into the world. 19I made myself holy on their behalf so that they also would be made holy in the truth.

John 17:20

20“I’m not praying only for them but also for those who believe in
me because of their word. 21I pray they will be one, Father, just as you
are in me and I am in you. I pray that they also will be in us, so that the
world will believe that you sent me. 22I’ve given them the glory that you
gave me so that they can be one just as we are one. 23I’m in them and
you are in me so that they will be made perfectly one. Then the world
will know that you sent me and that you have loved them just as you
loved me.

24“Father, I want those you gave me to be with me where I am. Then
they can see my glory, which you gave me because you loved me before
the creation of the world.

25“Righteous Father, even the world didn’t know you, but I’ve known
you, and these believers know that you sent me. 26I’ve made your name
known to them and will continue to make it known so that your love for
me will be in them, and I myself will be in them.”

Chapter Five

The Arrest, Trial, and Crucifixion of the King

Pilate said to the Jewish leaders, "Here's your king." The Jewish leaders cried out, "Take him away! Take him away! Crucify him!" Pilate responded, "What? Do you want me to crucify your king?" "We have no king except the emperor," the chief priests answered. Then Pilate handed Jesus over to be crucified. The soldiers took Jesus prisoner. Carrying his cross by himself, he went out to a place called Skull Place (in Aramaic, Golgotha*). That's where they crucified him—and two others with him, one on each side and Jesus in the middle. Pilate had a public notice written and posted on the cross. It read "Jesus the Nazarene, the king of the Jews." Many of the Jews read this sign, for the place where Jesus was crucified was near the city and it was written in Aramaic, Latin, and Greek. (John 19:14b-20)*

5

The Arrest, Trial, and Crucifixion of the King

The Gospel of John reaches its dramatic climax with the arrest, trial, and crucifixion of Jesus. One of the major themes in John's account is that it was precisely here, in his suffering, that Jesus was revealed to be the long-awaited messianic King, and it was here that we see his hour of glory as he suffered and died on the cross, giving himself to save the world.

There are at least two things that deserve close attention here. First, once again we find that the details of John's account differ in important ways from Matthew, Mark, and Luke. You might think, "Well, those are just little details that don't really matter." Wrong. As we've seen, the details matter in John, particularly when we find differences from the Synoptic Gospels. John likely was familiar with other accounts of Jesus' crucifixion. When he offers details that are different from what we might call the "standard account" of the Crucifixion, it's likely that he gives us clues or signs that point toward some deeper meaning or help reveal the significance of Jesus and the cross. So pay attention to the differences.

Second, the two major themes in John's account of the Crucifixion are the Passover and the kingship of Jesus. It is in this section of John that Christ is enthroned. As we noted before, in Matthew, Mark, and Luke the focus is on the kingdom of God, but in John the focus is on Jesus as King.

The Arrest of the King

It was late Thursday night of what came to be known as Holy Week. Jesus and his disciples left the upper room and made their way down Mount Zion. They passed the temple and walked through the Kidron Valley to a garden that the Synoptic Gospels call Gethsemane, at the base of the Mount of Olives. It was likely around midnight that they made this journey. There, in Gethsemane, Jesus was arrested. Let's take note of the differences in John's account of the arrest, as compared with the accounts of Matthew, Mark, and Luke.

When Matthew, Mark, and Luke describe Jesus' arrest, the focus is on Jesus' human agony. Mark tells us,

> He began to feel despair and was anxious. He said to them, "I'm very sad. It's as if I'm dying. Stay here and keep alert." Then he went a short distance farther and fell to the ground. He prayed that, if possible, he might be spared the time of suffering.
>
> (Mark 14:33b-35)

Matthew parallels Mark's account, and Luke adds that Jesus was in such anguish that his "sweat became like drops of blood falling on the ground" (Luke 22:44).

But John doesn't include any of this. He merely says, "Jesus went out with his disciples and crossed over to the other side of the Kidron Valley. He and his disciples entered a garden there" (John 18:1). Why doesn't John include the story of Jesus' anguish in the garden, or his prayers that "this cup pass from me" (Matthew 26:39 NRSV)?

It's because, in contrast to the Synoptic Gospels' focus on Jesus' humanity, John's Gospel stresses Jesus' divinity. John does not show Jesus in agony in the garden. He was a King firmly in control of his destiny. He was the Divine who, with strength and dignity, approached his destiny.

John does not show Jesus in agony in the garden. He was a King firmly in control of his destiny.

Only in John are we told that a cohort of armed Roman soldiers came to arrest the unarmed Jesus. A cohort was approximately six hundred soldiers (though the term could occasionally be used for as few as two hundred). Picture six hundred police officers showing up to arrest someone. John's mention of the size of the arresting force is likely intended to show the perceived threat Jesus represented. John reports what took place next:

> Jesus knew everything that was to happen to him, so he went out and asked, "Who are you looking for?" They answered,

> "Jesus the Nazarene." He said to them, "I Am." (Judas, his betrayer, was standing with them.) When he said, "I Am," they shrank back and fell to the ground. (18:4-6)

This detail is not found in Matthew, Mark, or Luke. We learned in Chapter 3 that the words "I Am" in Greek—*ego eimi*—are roughly equivalent to the Hebrew word *Yahweh*—a personal name for God that means "I am that I am" or "I am life (or being) itself." When Jesus spoke that name, the soldiers shrank back and fell to the ground. Why? What does John intend for us to understand by including this detail? Once more in this passage, Jesus was identifying with God, and at his words the soldiers retreated in fear. By depicting the scene in this way, John captures the authority, courage, and hidden identity of Jesus.

I'm reminded of a game I used to play with my children when they were small. They would come and tackle me, or wrap their arms and legs around my legs and say, "We've got you, Daddy!" But then I would pick them up and throw them over my shoulders and say, "Now, who has who?" The power and control had shifted.

In the garden, the six hundred soldiers shrank back as Jesus, the mighty King, willingly presented himself for arrest. This was hardly Jesus in anguish throwing himself to the ground, asking for the cup to pass from him, as he is portrayed in other Gospels. In fact, in John's account Jesus said to his disciples, "Am I not to drink the cup the Father has given me?" (John 18:11b). Both pictures of Jesus are important, but here John wants us to see Jesus' divinity and to understand that Jesus was in complete control of the situation.

THE TRIALS OF JESUS

Unlike what is described in Matthew, Mark, and Luke, in John's Gospel Jesus did not appear before the Sanhedrin, the Jewish ruling council. He appeared briefly before Annas, the former high priest, and again before Caiaphas, the reigning high priest, but very little is said about these trials except that the priests apparently agreed Jesus should be executed for claiming to be the Son of God. Then Jesus was bound over to Pontius Pilate, the Roman governor of Judea.

Pilate's job was to maintain the peace of Rome, making sure Rome's power was exerted in the land of Judea. The charge the high priest made against Jesus was insurrection—that he was claiming to be King of the Jews in rebellion against Caesar. Insurrection was a crime punishable by death.

This charge sets up the theme of Jesus' kingship. In John's account of Jesus' trial before Pilate and his crucifixion, the word *king* or *kingdom* is used fifteen times.

> Pilate went back into the palace. He summoned Jesus and asked, "Are you the king of the Jews?" Jesus answered, "Do you say this on your own or have others spoken to you about me?" Pilate responded, "I'm not a Jew, am I? Your nation and its chief priests handed you over to me. What have you done?" Jesus replied, "My kingdom doesn't originate from this world. If it did, my guards would fight so that I wouldn't have been arrested by the Jewish leaders. My kingdom isn't from here." "So you are a king?" Pilate said. Jesus answered, "You say that I am a king. I was born and came into the world for this reason: to testify to the truth. Whoever accepts the truth listens to my voice." (John 18:33-37)

John's account depicts Jesus as a King whose Kingdom is not like those of this world. It is a Kingdom that transcends geographic boundaries and even time. It is a Kingdom made up of all who believe in him, follow him, and seek to love God and neighbor. It is a Kingdom of truth, light, and life.

When John describes Jesus as King, his hope is to persuade his readers to accept Jesus as *their* King—for us to accept him as *our* King. His kingship comes before our earthly political allegiances.

A pastor friend of mine related a conversation he had with a parishioner about politics and faith. The man said to my friend, "We are Americans first and Christians second." That is precisely the opposite of what Jesus expects when he reveals himself to be King. He demands our *highest* allegiance.

My Jewish friends often address God in prayer with these words: "Blessed are You, Lord our God, King of the Universe. . . ." When we address Jesus as "Lord," we are using a term that reflects authority and rule. Caesar was addressed as Lord. John understands that Jesus is the Lord of lords. The earliest Christian creed, found in Romans 10:9 and First Corinthians 12:3, is "Jesus is Lord."

Those of us who are followers of Christ are actually citizens of two kingdoms. Most of us are citizens of the United States. We love our country and are willing to die for it. But the United States isn't going to last forever. The kingdom of God, by contrast, will last forever, and each of us will be part of this eternal Kingdom. So our primary allegiance is to Christ as our King and to the kingdom of God.

In Jesus' trial before Pontius Pilate, again and again Pilate said he found no basis for putting Jesus to death. But the crowd, including the religious leaders, demanded Jesus' crucifixion. Would Pilate do the right thing, or would he do the politically expedient thing? Pilate knew that the right thing was to release Jesus, but he didn't do it because he was afraid. What would it do to his career? What would it do to his stature?

In this account, Pilate represents all of us, because at some point in our lives we will face this trial and this test. What will we do when given that choice? Is it Christ or career? Christ or status? Christ or money? What is the trial you face?

Of course, in a very real sense this wasn't Jesus' trial at all; it was the trial of Pontius Pilate and the religious leaders. Pilate stood in conversation with the King of kings, sensed that this man was more than he seemed, and referred to him repeatedly as a king. Yet because of Pilate's concern for himself, he sent Christ to die. He may have helped his political career, but he failed the test.

This is an appropriate time to note that John repeatedly uses the phrase "the Jews" in his Gospel to describe those who oppose Jesus. In the Crucifixion scenes, it is "the Jews" who call for Jesus' crucifixion. The phrase is used twenty times in John, and almost always in a disparaging way toward the Jewish people. (The phrase only appears thirteen times in the other three gospels *combined*, and it is never used disparagingly.) Some scholars believe the reason John used the phrase disparagingly may have been because by the time he wrote, some of the Jewish leadership had begun excommunicating Jewish Christians from the synagogues.

When John speaks of "the Jews," clearly he is referring not to all Jews but just to some of the Jewish leadership. Throughout the Gospel, after all, most people who come to believe in Jesus are Jews. The disciples are Jews. Jesus himself is a Jew. In an attempt to draw a helpful distinction, the Common English Bible rightly recognizes that John's phrase is in reference to a small segment of the Jewish population and so translates the Greek phrase "the Jews" as "the Jewish leadership." But most translations take a more literal approach.

I mention this issue because throughout history John's use of the phrase in such a derogatory way (along with Luke's use of it in the Book of Acts) likely played some part in the anti-Semitism that has reared its head throughout church history. I am certain John would have been grieved over this misunderstanding, given that he himself was a Jew and likely so were most of his friends and family.

Some Christians may still repeat the statement that "the Jews killed Jesus." However, it was the Roman soldiers who crucified Jesus, at the urging of some of the Jewish leadership and perhaps some of the merchants whom Jesus had offended by casting them out of the Temple. To blame all Jews for the acts of a very small number is no more appropriate than saying all Christians are members of the Ku Klux Klan. One could rightly argue that no real Christians would be members of the KKK; likewise, any Jewish leaders who called for the crucifixion of an innocent man would not be faithful Jews.

Let's return to John's account of Jesus' trial and crucifixion. In many ways the story parallels the one found in Matthew, Mark, and Luke. But I want to focus on several differences regarding what one might think to be minor details. Remember, the details matter in John, and when there's a divergence from what we might call the normative tradition (the story as it came to be told by Matthew, Mark, and Luke), we may want to pay particular attention. Allow me to point out just a few of the details that are unique to John's Gospel.

Notice that in Matthew, Mark, and Luke, when Jesus is sent to be crucified he is unable to carry his own cross, hence Simon of Cyrene is pressed into service and forced to carry it instead. But in John we read, "The soldiers took Jesus prisoner. Carrying his cross by himself, he went out to a place called Skull Place (in Aramaic, *Golgotha*). That's where they crucified him" (John 19:16b-18a). Why did John emphasize that Jesus carried his own cross? Once again John seems to want us to see Jesus as the strong and dignified Son of God.

In crucifixion, the vertical portion of the cross, called the *stipe*, was kept at the site of the crucifixion. But victims were forced to carry the horizontal portion, a seventy-pound crossbeam, which in Latin is the *petibulum*, and it became the instrument of their own torture and death. In John's Gospel, Jesus picked up the heavy crossbeam with strength and intentionality, changing it into an instrument of salvation. It's as if Jesus was saying, "This is not only the instrument of my death but also of the fulfillment of my mission."

Jesus picked up the heavy crossbeam with strength and intentionality, changing it into an instrument of salvation. It's as if Jesus was saying, "This is not only the instrument of my death but also of the fulfillment of my mission."

Again we return to John's text: "It was about noon on the Preparation Day for the Passover" (19:14). In Matthew, Mark, and Luke, Jesus was crucified on the first day of the Passover in the morning. But John tells us Jesus was crucified at noon on the Preparation Day, one day before the first full day of Passover. As always in John, the differing details—in this case date and time—turn out to be important.[1]

When your Jewish friends celebrate the Passover, what are they commemorating? Thirteen hundred years before the birth of Jesus, the Israelites were slaves in Egypt. God sent Moses to convince Pharaoh that he should release the slaves, but Pharaoh refused. Then God sent plague after plague, trying to force Pharaoh to relent. Pharaoh still refused. The last of the plagues was the death of the firstborn children and animals throughout Egypt. On that night the angel of death would pass through Egypt, but God offered the Israelites a way to identify themselves as God's people and thus to be spared from this terrible plague. God told the Israelites to slaughter a lamb, roast it, and eat it. They were then to take some of the lamb's blood and, using a hyssop branch, sprinkle the blood of the lamb on their doorposts. The angel of death, seeing the blood, would pass over the Jewish houses, sparing their children and animals from death. That night, the Egyptians were so decimated by the plague that they released the Israelites and sent them away.

Following that night, God commanded Moses to have the Israelites mark their deliverance with a meal, the Passover Seder. Each year on the Day of Preparation, a day prior to Passover, the Jewish people would slaughter one lamb per household, and the meat would be roasted and shared in celebration of God's deliverance, salvation, and liberation.

In Matthew, Mark, and Luke, the Passover Seder is the Last Supper, and the lambs have been sacrificed and prepared earlier on the Day of Preparation. But in John, Jesus is crucified on the Day of Preparation. Why does John tell us that Jesus was crucified as the lambs were being slaughtered? Because he wants his readers to see Jesus as a kind of Passover lamb. In John 1:29 he has already introduced this theme when John the Baptist looks at Jesus and announces, "Look! The Lamb of God who takes away the sin of the world!"

On that first Passover, the lambs were slaughtered not to take away sin but to spare the firstborn of the Israelites from death. From that time on, the lambs were slaughtered at Passover as a visible reminder of God's deliverance of the Israelite children from death and of the Israelite people from slavery. This is part of what John wants his readers to see: Jesus, by his death, delivers us from slavery to sin, and he frees us from the fear and power of death.

Jesus, by his death, delivers us from slavery to sin, and he frees us from the fear and power of death.

How are we slaves to sin? The Apostle Paul captures it well when he writes, "I'm sold as a slave to sin. I don't know what I'm doing, because I don't do what I want to do. Instead, I do the thing that I hate" (Romans 7:14b-15). Sin seems to "own" us. But, like the death of the Passover lambs and the Israelites' liberation from slavery in Egypt, the death of Christ is intended to free us from slavery to sin.

John wants us to understand that Jesus, like the Passover lamb, liberates us from slavery and bondage. And Jesus frees us from death. There are many metaphors in the New Testament by which the apostles sought to explain the significance of Jesus' death, but for John this idea of liberation is essential. To make further sense of it, let's take a closer look at John's account of the Crucifixion.

THE CRUCIFIXION OF THE KING

> *The soldiers took Jesus prisoner. Carrying his cross by himself, he went out to a place called Skull Place (in Aramaic,* Golgotha*). That's where they crucified him—and two others with him, one on each side and Jesus in the middle. Pilate had a public notice written and posted on the cross. It read "Jesus the Nazarene, the king of the Jews." Many of the Jews read this sign, for the place where Jesus was crucified was near the city and it was written in Aramaic, Latin, and Greek. (John 19:16b-20)*

Notice the sign that was placed over Jesus' head. Every criminal who was crucified had a sign that named his crime. The sign over

Jesus read "Jesus the Nazarene, the king of the Jews." Only John tells us that this inscription was posted in three languages: Aramaic, the language of the Near East; Latin, the language of the West; and Greek, the language of the Hellenistic world.

Why does John tell us this? Because these were the languages of the Roman Empire; these were the languages of the world. In other words, in the very inscription meant to name Jesus' crime, the Roman governor inadvertently became the first to declare that Jesus is the King, not just to the Jews but to the whole world.

This detail leads to a really important idea for John, something that he's been driving toward for the entire Gospel: here, on the cross, Jesus is enthroned and his glory is revealed; he is a king who embraced death to save his people. We're meant to wonder and to reflect in awe: What kind of king would willingly give himself as a ransom, an offering of redemption, to save his people?

John goes on to tell us that as Jesus hung on the cross, those nearby offered him a drink of wine. They affixed a sponge to a hyssop branch, dipped it in sour wine, and raised it to his lips. Isn't it odd that John would feel the need to tell us the type of branch that was used?

But hyssop wasn't just any branch. Listen to Moses' instructions to the elders of Israel on the night of the first Passover:

> "Go pick out one of the flock for your families, and slaughter the Passover lamb. Take a bunch of hyssop, dip it into the blood that is in the bowl, and touch the beam above the door and the two doorposts with the blood in the bowl." (Exodus 12:21b-22a)

Hyssop was used to ensure that the children of Israel wouldn't die, even as they were being delivered from slavery! Once again, John is seeking to make it clear that Jesus came to liberate us and save us from death, and the hyssop branch is one of several clues and symbols John uses to that end.

But there was another use of hyssop in the Old Testament: hyssop branches were used in rites of purification (see Leviticus 14 and Numbers 19). It became associated with God's work in cleansing his people. Thus David would say, "Purify me with hyssop and I will be clean; wash me and I will be whiter than snow" (Psalm 51:7).

We find two things happening at the same time in John's version of the story. Jesus the Passover lamb sets us free from slavery, and Jesus the King sacrifices himself to purify God's people and to save them (us!) from sin and death. We look at the cross and ask: Exactly how does this work? How can someone who died two thousand years ago save us from our sins? It's okay to scratch your head. I certainly have at times in my life.

Sometimes you'll hear Christians say they've got it all figured out. They have a theory of atonement that explains it all, sort of like an equation in math. The sum weight of the world's sin is *x*. Jesus' righteousness is *y*. So *x* minus *y* results in our being forgiven.

I don't think Jesus' death works like that. To me, it's not math; it's more like poetry or a divine drama. The way we see the cross of Christ changes, like a kaleidoscope, at different times in our lives and affects us differently. At times his death is primarily about our need for forgiveness and his willingness to purify us. At other times the cross will convey God's power to liberate us from what enslaves us emotionally or spiritually. At still other times the cross becomes a reminder of the selfless love of our King, who laid down his life for his people.

A woman in our congregation once told me that her father had been drinking and driving and had killed a little girl. He went to prison, and after getting out he still could not forgive himself. I believe what he needed to know, as difficult as it might have been to accept, was that God had come in the person of Jesus Christ on the cross to bear the weight of the world's sins, including this man's.

A couple I know had been deeply hurt and couldn't forgive the person who had harmed them. They tried to let it go but instead replayed the offending act over and over again in their minds. It was not until they saw the other person's sin in the light of the cross that they were able to let go of their anger and pain. The cross liberated them from their hurt and their need for revenge.

Jesus sets us free from sin. On the cross, Christ both bears our sin and shows us the way of selfless love. We're slaves to our fear and our dread of death, but by his cross and resurrection he sets us free from these fears. Perhaps the single greatest form of slavery that many of us experience is our uncertainty that we are loved. Every one of us longs to be loved, and yet many of us have never experienced that certainty, especially not when we were growing up. It leads us to all kinds of behaviors in an effort to win love. It enslaves us.

Perhaps the single greatest form of slavery that many of us experience is our uncertainty that we are loved.

In his book *Proof of Heaven*, neurosurgeon Eben Alexander writes that he lay in a deep coma for seven days, and while there he had an experience of heaven. Alexander tells us at one point in his story that as a child he had been given up for adoption. Then, when he tried to make contact with his biological parents, they did not want to see him. Their rejection sent him into a depression. For seven years he struggled with something deep inside, feeling convinced he was not wanted or loved by those who gave him life. Here he was, a successful neurosurgeon with a family of his own, struggling with a deep-seated need to know that he was loved. And yet it's part of what Christ showed us most clearly when he died on the cross: the depth of God's love and the value God places on our lives.

When my children were small, I knew of no other way to express the depth of my love than to say, "I love you so much that I would give my life for you." That's what Christ was showing us and modeling for us. This love of the King is why the Crucifixion was his hour of glorification. In it, he was showing us the depth of God's love.

I read a news story out of Afghanistan several years ago. An Afghan police officer named Murad Khan saw a suicide bomber coming toward his guard station. There were children all around. He ran and wrapped his arms around the man just as the bomb was detonated. Khan and eight children were killed.[2] However, many more were saved by this man who thought less of his own life than of the children around him. He gave up everything to save them. What an amazing picture of sacrificial love. I wonder how his death affected those who survived because of his sacrifice.

I think of Donald Liu, a pediatric surgeon in Chicago, who saved two little boys who were being pulled into the undertow on Lake Michigan. He jumped in to save them. He managed to get them to safety but died in doing so.[3]

The actions of Khan, Liu, and others are great examples of heroism, and the self-giving love embodied in those acts offers hints of the glory John saw when Jesus, the High King of Heaven, embraced the cross to demonstrate God's love, to redeem us from sin, to reconcile us to God, to save us from ourselves.

Let's conclude with Jesus' final words from the cross. In Matthew and Mark, his only words from the cross were, "My God, my God, why have you forsaken me?" (Matthew 27:46 NRSV). But John does not record these words. Jesus did not question God. He was injured and suffering, yet strong and determined.

In John, the final words of Jesus were "It is finished" (John 19:30 NRSV). I had often interpreted those words to mean that Christ was exhausted and defeated. But then I learned that in Greek the phrase is expressed in just one word: *tetelestai*. That word is a shout of victory announcing that a battle has been won, a mission accomplished. As William H. Willimon has suggested, it's what Michelangelo might have shouted after his final brushstroke on the ceiling of the Sistine Chapel. Standing below, looking up at his masterpiece, Michelangelo could have shouted, "*It* is finished!"[5] Surely Jesus' final words carried that same meaning. A masterpiece had been completed. God's saving mission was finished.

John intends for us to see that on the cross God has come to us, taking the hate, the hurt, the sin of the world. There Jesus is the Word, and the Word conveys the utter brokenness of the human race, who, when God walked the earth, nailed him to a cross. But the Word also conveys that God suffers for the human race, that God is willing to show us mercy, to save us, and to liberate us. Finally, the Word that is Jesus conveys the depth of God's love for humanity. This is where we see God's glory. This scene, Christ crucified, rightly understood, is God's masterpiece.

Lord, I need what you have done on the cross. I need your mercy offered there. Please purify me and forgive me. I need to be saved from myself and from my sin. Liberate me from the things that enslave me. And help me to see, in Jesus' death on the cross, your selfless love for me. Thank you, Lord, for your glorious cross! Amen.

The Gospel of John: Part Five

John 18–19 (CEB)

As you read John 18–19 you will explore John's account of the arrest, trial, and crucifixion of the King.

John 17:20
[20]“I’m not praying only for them but also for those who believe in
me because of their word. [21]I pray they will be one, Father, just as you
are in me and I am in you. I pray that they also will be in us, so that the
world will believe that you sent me. [22]I’ve given them the glory that you
gave me so that they can be one just as we are one. [23]I’m in them and
you are in me so that they will be made perfectly one. Then the world
will know that you sent me and that you have loved them just as you
loved me.
[24]“Father, I want those you gave me to be with me where I am. Then
glory, which you gave me because you loved me before
e world.
ther, even the world didn’t know you, but I’ve known
lievers know that you sent me. [26]I’ve made your name
d will continue to make it known so that your love for
em, and I myself will be in them.”

START THIS WEEK’S READING AT CHAPTER 18

Arrest in the garden

18 After he said these things, Jesus went out with his disciples and
crossed over to the other side of the Kidron Valley. He and his disciples entered a garden there. [2]Judas, his betrayer, also knew the place
because Jesus often gathered there with his disciples. [3]Judas brought a
company of soldiers[a] and some guards from the chief priests and Pharisees. They came there carrying lanterns, torches, and weapons. [4]Jesus
knew everything that was to happen to him, so he went out and asked,
“Who are you looking for?”
[5]They answered, “Jesus the Nazarene.”
He said to them, “I Am.”[b] (Judas, his betrayer, was standing with
them.) [6]When he said, “I Am,” they shrank back and fell to the ground.
[7]He asked them again, “Who are you looking for?”
They said, “Jesus the Nazarene.”
[8]Jesus answered, “I told you, ‘I Am.’[c] If you are looking for me, then
let these people go.” [9]This was so that the word he had spoken might be
fulfilled: “I didn’t lose anyone of those whom you gave me.”
[10]Then Simon Peter, who had a sword, drew it and struck the high
priest’s servant, cutting off his right ear. (The servant’s name was
Malchus.) [11]Jesus told Peter, “Put your sword away! Am I not to drink
the cup the Father has given me?” [12]Then the company of soldiers,
the commander, and the guards from the Jewish leaders took Jesus
into custody. They bound him [13]and led him first to Annas. He was the
father-in-law of Caiaphas, the high priest that year. ([14]Caiaphas was

[a]Or *cohort* (approximately six hundred soldiers) [b]Or *It is I* [c]Or *It is I*

the one who had advised the Jewish leaders that it was better for one
person to die for the people.)

Peter denies Jesus

15Simon Peter and another disciple followed Jesus. Because this other
disciple was known to the high priest, he went with Jesus into the high
priest's courtyard. 16However, Peter stood outside near the gate. Then
the other disciple (the one known to the high priest) came out and
spoke to the woman stationed at the gate, and she brought Peter in.
17The servant woman stationed at the gate asked Peter, "Aren't you one
of this man's disciples?"

"I'm not," he replied. 18The servants and the guards had made a fire
because it was cold. They were standing around it, warming themselves.
Peter joined them there, standing by the fire and warming himself.

Jesus testifies

19Meanwhile, the chief priest questioned Jesus about his disciples
and his teaching. 20Jesus answered, "I've spoken openly to the world.
I've always taught in synagogues and in the temple, where all the Jews
gather. I've said nothing in private. 21Why ask me? Ask those who heard
what I told them. They know what I said."

22After Jesus spoke, one of the guards standing there slapped Jesus
in the face. "Is that how you would answer the high priest?" he asked.

23Jesus replied, "If I speak wrongly, testify about what was wrong.
But if I speak correctly, why do you strike me?" 24Then Annas sent him,
bound, to Caiaphas the high priest.

Peter denies Jesus again

25Meanwhile, Simon Peter was still standing with the guards, warming himself. They asked, "Aren't you one of his disciples?"

Peter denied it, saying, "I'm not."

26A servant of the high priest, a relative of the one whose ear Peter
had cut off, said to him, "Didn't I see you in the garden with him?"
27Peter denied it again, and immediately a rooster crowed.

Trial before Pilate

28The Jewish leaders led Jesus from Caiaphas to the Roman governor's palace.[d] It was early in the morning. So that they could eat the Passover, the Jewish leaders wouldn't enter the palace; entering the palace would have made them ritually impure.

[d]Or *praetorium*

John 18:29

29 So Pilate went out to them and asked, “What charge do you bring against this man?”

30 They answered, “If he had done nothing wrong, we wouldn’t have handed him over to you.”

31 Pilate responded, “Take him yourselves and judge him according to your Law.”

The Jewish leaders replied, “The Law doesn’t allow us to kill anyone.” (32 This was so that Jesus’ word might be fulfilled when he indicated how he was going to die.)

Pilate questions Jesus

33 Pilate went back into the palace. He summoned Jesus and asked, “Are you the king of the Jews?”

34 Jesus answered, “Do you say this on your own or have others spoken to you about me?”

35 Pilate responded, “I’m not a Jew, am I? Your nation and its chief priests handed you over to me. What have you done?”

36 Jesus replied, “My kingdom doesn’t originate from this world. If it did, my guards would fight so that I wouldn’t have been arrested by the Jewish leaders. My kingdom isn’t from here.”

37 “So you are a king?” Pilate said.

Jesus answered, “You say that I am a king. I was born and came into the world for this reason: to testify to the truth. Whoever accepts the truth listens to my voice.”

38 “What is truth?” Pilate asked.

Release of Barabbas

After Pilate said this, he returned to the Jewish leaders and said, “I find no grounds for any charge against him. 39 You have a custom that I release one prisoner for you at Passover. Do you want me to release for you the king of the Jews?”

40 They shouted, “Not this man! Give us Barabbas!” (Barabbas was an outlaw.)

Jesus is whipped and mocked as king

19 Then Pilate had Jesus taken and whipped. 2 The soldiers twisted together a crown of thorns and put it on his head, and dressed him in a purple robe. 3 Over and over they went up to him and said, “Greetings, king of the Jews!” And they slapped him in the face.

4 Pilate came out of the palace again and said to the Jewish leaders, “Look! I’m bringing him out to you to let you know that I find no grounds for a charge against him.” 5 When Jesus came out, wearing

the crown of thorns and the purple robe, Pilate said to them, "Here's the man."

6When the chief priests and their deputies saw him, they shouted out, "Crucify, crucify!"

Pilate told them, "You take him and crucify him. I don't find any grounds for a charge against him."

7The Jewish leaders replied, "We have a Law, and according to this Law he ought to die because he made himself out to be God's Son."

Pilate questions Jesus again

8When Pilate heard this word, he was even more afraid. 9He went back into the residence and spoke to Jesus, "Where are you from?" Jesus didn't answer. 10So Pilate said, "You won't speak to me? Don't you know that I have authority to release you and also to crucify you?"

11Jesus replied, "You would have no authority over me if it had not been given to you from above. That's why the one who handed me over to you has the greater sin." 12From that moment on, Pilate wanted to release Jesus.

However, the Jewish leaders cried out, saying, "If you release this man, you aren't a friend of the emperor! Anyone who makes himself out to be a king opposes the emperor!"

13When Pilate heard these words, he led Jesus out and seated him on the judge's bench at the place called Stone Pavement (in Aramaic, *Gabbatha*). 14It was about noon on the Preparation Day for the Passover. Pilate said to the Jewish leaders, "Here's your king."

15The Jewish leaders cried out, "Take him away! Take him away! Crucify him!"

Pilate responded, "What? Do you want me to crucify your king?"

"We have no king except the emperor," the chief priests answered. 16Then Pilate handed Jesus over to be crucified.

Crucifixion

The soldiers took Jesus prisoner. 17Carrying his cross by himself, he went out to a place called Skull Place (in Aramaic, *Golgotha*). 18That's where they crucified him—and two others with him, one on each side and Jesus in the middle. 19Pilate had a public notice written and posted on the cross. It read "Jesus the Nazarene, the king of the Jews." 20Many of the Jews read this sign, for the place where Jesus was crucified was near the city and it was written in Aramaic, Latin, and Greek. 21Therefore, the Jewish chief priests complained to Pilate, "Don't write, 'The king of the Jews' but 'This man said, "I am the king of the Jews."'"

22Pilate answered, "What I've written, I've written."

John 19:23

[23]When the soldiers crucified Jesus, they took his clothes and his sandals, and divided them into four shares, one for each soldier. His shirt was seamless, woven as one piece from the top to the bottom. [24]They said to each other, "Let's not tear it. Let's cast lots to see who will get it." This was to fulfill the scripture,

They divided my clothes among themselves,
and they cast lots for my clothing.[e]

That's what the soldiers did.

[25]Jesus' mother and his mother's sister, Mary the wife of Clopas, and Mary Magdalene stood near the cross. [26]When Jesus saw his mother and the disciple whom he loved standing nearby, he said to his mother, "Woman, here is your son." [27]Then he said to the disciple, "Here is your mother." And from that time on, this disciple took her into his home.

[28]After this, knowing that everything was already completed, in order to fulfill the scripture, Jesus said, "I am thirsty." [29]A jar full of sour wine was nearby, so the soldiers soaked a sponge in it, placed it on a hyssop branch, and held it up to his lips. [30]When he had received the sour wine, Jesus said, "It is completed." Bowing his head, he gave up his life.

Witness at the cross

[31]It was the Preparation Day and the Jewish leaders didn't want the bodies to remain on the cross on the Sabbath, especially since that Sabbath was an important day. So they asked Pilate to have the legs of those crucified broken and the bodies taken down. [32]Therefore, the soldiers came and broke the legs of the two men who were crucified with Jesus. [33]When they came to Jesus, they saw that he was already dead so they didn't break his legs. [34]However, one of the soldiers pierced his side with a spear, and immediately blood and water came out. [35]The one who saw this has testified, and his testimony is true. He knows that he speaks the truth, and he has testified so that you also can believe. [36]These things happened to fulfill the scripture, *They won't break any of his bones.*[f] [37]And another scripture says, *They will look at him whom they have pierced.*[g]

Jesus' body is buried

[38]After this Joseph of Arimathea asked Pilate if he could take away the body of Jesus. Joseph was a disciple of Jesus, but a secret one because he feared the Jewish authorities. Pilate gave him permission, so he came and took the body away. [39]Nicodemus, the one who at first had come to Jesus at night, was there too. He brought a mixture of myrrh

[e]Ps 22:18 [f]Exod 12:46 [g]Zech 12:10

and aloe, nearly seventy-five pounds in all.[h] 40Following Jewish burial
customs, they took Jesus' body and wrapped it, with the spices, in linen
cloths. 41There was a garden in the place where Jesus was crucified, and
in the garden was a new tomb in which no one had ever been laid. 42Be-
cause it was the Jewish Preparation Day and the tomb was nearby, they
laid Jesus in it.

[h] Or *one hundred litra*; that is, one hundred Roman pounds

Chapter Six

Eternal Life

There was a garden in the place where Jesus was crucified, and in the garden was a new tomb in which no one had ever been laid. Because it was the Jewish Preparation Day and the tomb was nearby, they laid Jesus in it. Early in the morning of the first day of the week, while it was still dark, Mary Magdalene came to the tomb and saw that the stone had been taken away from the tomb. . . . Mary stood outside near the tomb, crying. As she cried, she bent down to look into the tomb. She saw two angels dressed in white, seated where the body of Jesus had been, one at the head and one at the foot. The angels asked her, "Woman, why are you crying?" She replied, "They have taken away my Lord, and I don't know where they've put him." As soon as she had said this, she turned around and saw Jesus standing there, but she didn't know it was Jesus. Jesus said to her, "Woman, why are you crying? Who are you looking for?" Thinking he was the gardener, she replied, "Sir, if you have carried him away, tell me where you have put him and I will get him." Jesus said to her, "Mary." She turned and said to him in Aramaic, "Rabbouni" (which means Teacher*). . . . Mary Magdalene left and announced to the disciples, "I've seen the Lord." Then she told them what he said to her. (John 19:41–20:1, 11-16, 18)*

6

Eternal Life

At Easter we celebrate the resurrection of Jesus Christ. But we don't just celebrate his resurrection; we remember and celebrate what the event means. The Resurrection is a vindication of Christ's ministry, a confirmation of his identity, a validation of what he said and did. The Resurrection proclaims that evil and sin and even death will not have the final word. And, as Christians often say at Easter, the Resurrection declares that the worst thing is never the last thing. This is a message that seizes our hearts and continues to shape us and give us hope to the present day.

In this final chapter, we will focus on John's account of the first Easter. Christ's resurrection gives us a glimpse into the hope we have in our own resurrection and the fact that life eternal is available to us. That's the first part of the chapter. Then we'll turn to what Easter calls forth from us, what it demands of us every day if we're followers of Jesus Christ. Easter is not just a gift and a blessing. If we fully understand it, Easter asks something of us in response.

SORROW TO JOY AND HOPE, FEAR TO PEACE AND COURAGE

Let's begin with the touching story of Mary Magdalene coming to the tomb. Her life had been changed forever by her encounters with Jesus. Mary Magdalene was likely a single woman, which we can surmise from her name. In the first century, if a woman was married, she would often be identified as Mary, wife of.... If she had children she might be Mary the mother of.... But this Mary was referred to as Mary Magdalene—that is, Mary of Magdala, a town on the northwest coast of the Sea of Galilee.

Not only was Mary likely a single woman; she was a woman who had had a troubled past. Luke tells us that she had had "seven demons" (Luke 8:2). A demon in the first century could be anything from an unexplained physical illness to a psychiatric disorder to an addiction of some kind. It also could indicate a deep spiritual wrestling that might have involved an actual spiritual entity. Any of these meanings could have been covered by the word *demon*.

Whatever had afflicted Mary, she was a troubled person until she met Jesus, who set her free from the demons. She seems to have had some financial means despite the demons that had plagued her, because after her deliverance at Jesus' hands she is named as one of several women who followed Jesus and the disciples wherever they went and supplied some of the financial resources that made their ministry possible (see Luke 8:1-3).

I've always loved Mary's song in *Jesus Christ Superstar*, "I Don't Know How to Love Him." It captures what must have been the range of feelings Mary had for Jesus. He had utterly changed her life.

It is not hard to imagine just how deeply she loved him. Her love and courageous devotion to him were shown by her presence at the cross (John 19:25), by her accompanying his body to the grave (recorded in each of the Synoptics), and by her being the first to arrive at his tomb on Easter morning.

She came to the cemetery at dawn on Sunday morning—weeping, her faith in tatters, her heart broken. She couldn't stay away, but she was full of sorrow. Twice John tells us that she wept as she stood there, and as she did, she represented each of us who has lost someone we love dearly. We've all known Mary's sadness—the grief that comes in waves, and the tears that won't stop. If the death is untimely or unjust, as Jesus' death was, the sorrow is even greater. Our hearts break. We weep as Mary wept for this man who had loved her and whom she dearly loved.

I think of a two-week period at our church when we had sixteen deaths that were unrelated except for the common grief experienced by those left behind. The deceased included parents and grandparents, sisters and brothers, spouses, and even a four-year-old girl.

At these moments of death, in the midst of our grief, we urgently want to know: Is there something more? Is there such a thing as life after death? If so, what is it like? In John's Gospel, Mary represents each of us as she weeps at Jesus' tomb. John's account of the resurrection is in part a demonstration of Christ's triumph over the grave, and the hope we have for life beyond death.

THE ANGELS INSIDE THE TOMB

In John's account of the Resurrection, Mary looked inside the tomb and saw two angels. I want to pause for a moment at this point in the story to consider some unique features of John's account.

In each of the Gospel descriptions of the empty tomb, there is at least one angel. (The word in Greek means "messenger," and these would look like people. In fact, Mark simply describes a young man dressed in white.) In John's account there is an interesting detail included. He tells us there are two angels, and they are sitting inside the tomb on the ledge "where the body of Jesus had been, one at the head and one at the foot" (20:12).

Why does John tell us the angels were sitting? Further, why does he tell us the precise location where they were sitting (at the head and the foot of the place Jesus had been)?

I believe these details are an allusion to the so-called mercy seat of God—that is, the lid of the Ark of the Covenant, as described in the Book of Exodus. This "seat" was God's symbolic throne on earth. It was the place where God's covenant with Israel was kept. (The Ten Commandments were under the lid.) In Exodus 25:22, God said to Moses, "There I will meet with you." Once a year the high priest was to slaughter a bull and a lamb on behalf of the people, and he was to take some of the blood and sprinkle it on the mercy seat. This seat was constructed with an angel on either end.

Is it possible that John, in describing the angels in Jesus' tomb, is trying to point us to the meaning of Jesus' death and resurrection? Was he hoping we would see that this place where Jesus' body had lain was the new mercy seat and that here, by his own blood, Christ had reconciled humanity to God?

What Is Heaven Like?

Different religions and philosophies offer very different answers to the question of death. Christianity's answer to death is Easter (or perhaps better said, *God's* answer to death is Easter). The resurrection of Jesus is God's emphatic way of saying that death is not the end—that, in the words of Paul, "Death has been swallowed up in victory" (1 Corinthians 15:54 NRSV). Easter transforms our sorrow into joy and hope, our fear into peace and courage. This is what happened to Mary and the disciples on that first Easter.

The resurrection of Jesus is God's emphatic way of saying that death is not the end.

Jesus had been foreshadowing his resurrection throughout the Gospel of John. In John 5:28-29 he said,

> "Don't be surprised by this, because the time is coming when all who are in their graves will hear his voice. Those who did good things will come out into the resurrection of life, and those who did wicked things into the resurrection of judgment."

In 11:25-26 he promised,

> "I am the resurrection and the life. Whoever believes in me will live, even though they die. Everyone who lives and believes in me will never die."

In 14:1-3, just before he was arrested, he said to his disciples,

> "Don't be troubled. Trust in God. Trust also in me. My Father's house has room to spare. If that weren't the case, would I have told you that I'm going to prepare a place for you? When I go to prepare a place for you, I will return and take you to be with me so that where I am you will be too."

But as moving and hope-filled as Jesus' earlier statements had been, it was in the Resurrection itself that his words were powerfully demonstrated to be true. Jesus' resurrection demonstrated his power over death. Christians are not the only ones looking ahead to an afterlife. An increasing interest in the topic is reflected in the number of books about it that have sold millions of copies. There is the previously mentioned *Proof of Heaven*, by neurosurgeon Eben Alexander, as well as Todd Burpo's book *Heaven Is for Real* and many others. As a pastor, I often hear about near-death experiences of parishioners who tell me they have glimpsed heaven.

A woman in our congregation was in the hospital with a very serious illness; in fact, she nearly died twice. On one of those occasions, she felt herself slipping away, and suddenly she was somewhere else. This is how she described it:

> I began to see everyone that I knew who had died. The crowd was standing on both sides of the entrance as far as I could see. Everyone was clapping, waving their arms, and jumping up and down.... They were so glad to see me and I them... especially my parents. I cannot even describe the beauty of the river, the flowers and trees beside the water... there are no words except to say that it was beyond description... beautiful, sweet, awesome... the atmosphere was so happy. Believe me, this description seems so inadequate.

When the doctors began to bring her back, she remembers wanting to cry out, "No, please! I want to stay!" Afterward, because of that experience, she said, "I have no fear of dying now."

A fellow pastor shared with me his father's near-death experience:

> Dad was in a field, a beautiful green field out in the countryside. A most beautiful place. He did not want to leave. Time did not

> exist, he had nowhere to go, but wanted to just dwell in the peace. . . . As he lay down in the field, nearby he heard a stream of water, and off in the distance he heard my grandpa laughing and laughing. Dad said, "Grandpa was so happy." As Dad sat up, he saw a figure coming toward him. . . . It was Christ. . . . Jesus said to Dad, "Thomas, I am returning you to the prayers of the faithful."

I love that image of his grandfather, laughing off in the distance.

I have dozens more stories just like these that I could share. I believe they testify to what Jesus taught, what Mary saw, and what the disciples experienced that first Easter.

The Impact of Easter

In John's Gospel, Jesus or John mentions life or eternal life forty-seven times. That's more than Matthew, Mark, and Luke combined. So clearly this is a big idea for John. As I noted earlier, when Jesus spoke about eternal life, he always described it not as a future state after we die, but as something we begin to experience in the present.

According to Jesus, eternal life starts now. I think that means that if we know that Christ is the I Am, if we accept him as our King, if we recognize the significance of his death, and if we trust in his resurrection, we see and experience God's intention for human life *now*. This Word from God, this message embodied in Jesus' life, teachings, death, and resurrection, once accepted, changes everything. It is life-giving.

The Resurrection and its promise of life after death show that evil, sickness, and even death will not have the final word. Christ's promise in John 14:19—"Because I live, you will live too"—fundamentally changes how I face the deaths of people I love, how much risk I'm willing to take in my life, how I approach growing old, and how I look at my own death. I'm okay with death, at least my own. The older we get, and the more of our loved ones are on the other side, the more we're meant to look forward to that great reunion. Of course we feel sorrow, we cry, and we grieve. But we do so as those who have hope.

I'm in my fifties now, and though our church has an active member who will celebrate his 106th birthday before this book is published, it is likely that I have fewer years ahead of me than I have behind me. When I'm sixty-five or seventy, it means I will have finished two-thirds of my life and will have only one-third left. If you're convinced that this life is the end, then every day you march closer to death is more depressing than the day before. Right? Yes, but not for those of us who believe that when you get to the end of this life, you've really just begun to live! I love how it is expressed in the *Hymn of Promise*:

> In our end is our beginning; in our time, infinity...
> In our death, a resurrection; at the last, a victory.[1]

In the United States, health care is one of the great crises of our time. We incur a large portion of health care costs in the last year of people's lives. In fact, we'll spend trillions of dollars over the next ten years trying to keep people alive an extra six months or three months or even just a week. In some situations this may be the right thing to do. But it seems to me that what we're facing is not so much a crisis in health care as it is a crisis of faith. We're not sure what we think about death, so we cling desperately to life. We spend everything we've got and try every heroic procedure available so we can stay alive or keep our loved ones alive for just one more day. I believe it's at least in part because we're not sure what happens after this life is over.

When I get to the end of my life, I want to be able to say I've had a good run, I've fought the good fight, and I'm ready to see what's on the other side of death's door. I hope to tell my children that it's okay to let me go. This doesn't mean I want to die. I don't look forward to it. I'm not hoping for it to happen anytime soon. But I've told my wife on many occasions that if I die tomorrow, I not only have had a great life, but I know death is not the end, and we will see one another again because I actually trust in Jesus' words and his resurrection as portrayed in John.

That's what Easter does for us when we claim Christ's resurrection and allow it to seize us. We can sing with Eliza E. Hewitt, the gospel songwriter who in 1898 penned these words:

> When we all get to heaven,
> what a day of rejoicing that will be.
> When we all see Jesus,
> we'll sing and shout the victory![2]

I've been asked if I would still be a Christian were it not for the promise of heaven. The answer is a resounding yes! I am a follower of Jesus Christ not because he is my ticket to heaven, but because I believe he is the way, the truth, and the life. Like the disciples, I believe his words offer the key to life. I find myself most fully alive when I am closest to him or when I am doing his work. When I reflect on the times in my life when I believe I've done the right thing, it's always something that Jesus taught me to do or that I've done in his name. When I think about the problems that face our world, I believe so many of them would be resolved if people practiced what Jesus taught: if they actually loved one another, if they saw greatness in servanthood, if they showed compassion, told the truth, practiced forgiveness, stopped judging, loved their enemies, and lived the Golden Rule.

I am a follower of Jesus Christ not because he is my ticket to heaven, but because I believe he is the way, the truth, and the life.

Yes, I would follow Jesus whether there was a heaven or not. But I am grateful there is a heaven and life after death.

THE GARDEN AND THE MISSION OF EASTER

There's one final point I want you to notice in John's account of Easter, one that John has hidden but hopes we will find. Let's return to John's account of the Resurrection: "There was a garden in the place where Jesus was crucified, and in the garden was a new tomb in which no one had ever been laid" (19:41).

As we've studied the Gospel of John, we've learned there is always more than meets the eye when John tells the story of Christ. A little detail in verse 41 seems important to John. He mentions that there was a garden where Jesus was crucified, and then he says "in the garden there was a new tomb." Matthew, Mark, and Luke don't tell us there was a garden where Jesus was crucified, nor where he was buried. These details provide a clue, not just to John's view of the Resurrection but to John's approach throughout his account of Jesus' life.

Remember, John's Gospel opens with the words "In the beginning," the same words that open the Book of Genesis. Genesis starts in a garden. John's Gospel ends in a garden. In Genesis, God plants the garden. In John, when Mary Magdalene stands at the empty tomb and first sees the resurrected Christ, she thinks he is the gardener.

To delve a bit deeper, in Genesis Adam and Eve turn from God, eat of the forbidden fruit, and paradise is lost. They are expelled from the garden. The earth is placed under a curse, and death comes into the world. I read this story as archetypal: it is our story. Each of us hears the serpent's whisper. Each of us has turned from God's path, has done what we know is wrong, and death and pain result.

What is John hinting at by taking us back to the beginning? Why does he tell us Jesus was crucified and buried in a garden, and after being raised he appeared as a gardener? I believe John wants us to understand that Jesus came to break the curse, to destroy death, and to heal God's garden. Paul describes Jesus as the "second Adam." Perhaps that same idea is what John has in mind here. The first Adam ruined Paradise; the second Adam restored it. To put it another way, perhaps God the gardener, who took on flesh in Jesus' birth, death, and resurrection, has gone about setting the world aright. He has come to repair the garden.

But God's work was only begun in Jesus' resurrection. We still live in a world afflicted with violence, materialism, deception, and worse. There's work yet to be done. This is why, on the night when the risen Christ finally appeared to his disciples, he breathed on them and said, "As the father sent me, so I am sending you" (John 20:21). What Jesus began, we're meant to complete.

During his ministry as described in the Gospels, Jesus spent very little time teaching people about heaven. Most of what he taught was about how we should live to create a bit of heaven on earth. Two of his best-loved parables, the Good Samaritan and the sheep and goats, focus on our responsibility to care for those in need. His Sermon on the Mount barely mentions heaven but instead strongly challenges us to live by heaven's ethics here on earth, practicing love, justice, and reconciliation.

Our work is to follow Jesus in restoring the garden. That means that every day we are on a mission. Every morning we wake and say, "Here I am, Lord. Send me!" Every conversation we have, every decision we make, every action we take is an opportunity for God's kingdom to come on earth as it is in heaven.

Every conversation we have, every decision we make, every action we take is an opportunity for God's kingdom to come on earth as it is in heaven.

Each year at Easter, our church commits a significant portion of the Easter offering to one or two projects that will heal our city—that will restore the garden. We provide beds for children who are sleeping on the floor, jobs for men just out of prison, housing for people moving away from homelessness. We give such grants each year from the Easter offering, in part because we believe Easter is about restoring God's garden.

We proclaim it every Easter: Christ is risen from the grave! Death is swallowed up in victory! Sin and evil will never have the final word! The curse is broken! There is always hope!

POSTSCRIPT

In this little book, we've just scratched the surface of John's Gospel. We've learned a bit about how John writes. We've covered some of the major themes John offers us. We've explored the way Jesus brings us light and life. And we've come to understand who Jesus is to John, and who he can be to us. We've also had the opportunity to read the entire Gospel of John on our own.

In closing, I remind you once again of John's stated intent in writing the Gospel, as noted in 20:30-31:

> Jesus did many other miraculous signs in his disciples' presence, signs that aren't recorded in this scroll. But these things are written so that you will believe that Jesus is the Christ, God's Son, and that believing, you will have life in his name.

May you believe and find light and life in Christ's name.

Lord Jesus, help me not only to believe in you, but also to trust in you. Thank you for John's testimony and for the way it helps me to see who you are and who you call me to be. May I, like Mary Magdalene and those first witnesses to the resurrection, be filled with your light and life. Amen.

The Gospel of John: Part Six

John 20–21 (CEB)

In John 20–21 you come to the dramatic conclusion of John's Gospel with the account of Jesus' resurrection and his subsequent conversations with his disciples.

John 19:40

START THIS WEEK'S READING AT CHAPTER 20

…eventy-five pounds in all.[h] 40Following Jewish burial …k Jesus' body and wrapped it, with the spices, in linen … a garden in the place where Jesus was crucified, and …a new tomb in which no one had ever been laid. 42Be… …wish Preparation Day and the tomb was nearby, they …

Empty tomb

20 Early in the morning of the first day of the week, while it was still dark, Mary Magdalene came to the tomb and saw that the stone had been taken away from the tomb. 2She ran to Simon Peter and the other disciple, the one whom Jesus loved, and said, "They have taken the Lord from the tomb, and we don't know where they've put him." 3Peter and the other disciple left to go to the tomb. 4They were running together, but the other disciple ran faster than Peter and was the first to arrive at the tomb. 5Bending down to take a look, he saw the linen cloths lying there, but he didn't go in. 6Following him, Simon Peter entered the tomb and saw the linen cloths lying there. 7He also saw the face cloth that had been on Jesus' head. It wasn't with the other clothes but was folded up in its own place. 8Then the other disciple, the one who arrived at the tomb first, also went inside. He saw and believed. 9They didn't yet understand the scripture that Jesus must rise from the dead. 10Then the disciples returned to the place where they were staying.

Jesus appears to Mary

11Mary stood outside near the tomb, crying. As she cried, she bent down to look into the tomb. 12She saw two angels dressed in white, seated where the body of Jesus had been, one at the head and one at the foot. 13The angels asked her, "Woman, why are you crying?"

She replied, "They have taken away my Lord, and I don't know where they've put him." 14As soon as she had said this, she turned around and saw Jesus standing there, but she didn't know it was Jesus.

15Jesus said to her, "Woman, why are you crying? Who are you looking for?"

Thinking he was the gardener, she replied, "Sir, if you have carried him away, tell me where you have put him and I will get him."

16Jesus said to her, "Mary."

She turned and said to him in Aramaic, "Rabbouni" (which means *Teacher*).

[h] Or *one hundred litra*; that is, one hundred Roman pounds

17 Jesus said to her, "Don't hold on to me, for I haven't yet gone up to
my Father. Go to my brothers and sisters and tell them, 'I'm going up
to my Father and your Father, to my God and your God.'"
18 Mary Magdalene left and announced to the disciples, "I've seen the
Lord." Then she told them what he said to her.

Jesus appears to the disciples

19 It was still the first day of the week. That evening, while the disciples were behind closed doors because they were afraid of the Jewish
authorities, Jesus came and stood among them. He said, "Peace be with
you." 20 After he said this, he showed them his hands and his side. When
the disciples saw the Lord, they were filled with joy. 21 Jesus said to them
again, "Peace be with you. As the Father sent me, so I am sending you."
22 Then he breathed on them and said, "Receive the Holy Spirit. 23 If you
forgive anyone's sins, they are forgiven; if you don't forgive them, they
aren't forgiven."

Jesus appears to Thomas and the disciples

24 Thomas, the one called Didymus,[i] one of the Twelve, wasn't with
the disciples when Jesus came. 25 The other disciples told him, "We've
seen the Lord!"
But he replied, "Unless I see the nail marks in his hands, put my finger in the wounds left by the nails, and put my hand into his side, I
won't believe."
26 After eight days his disciples were again in a house and Thomas was
with them. Even though the doors were locked, Jesus entered and stood
among them. He said, "Peace be with you." 27 Then he said to Thomas,
"Put your finger here. Look at my hands. Put your hand into my side.
No more disbelief. Believe!"
28 Thomas responded to Jesus, "My Lord and my God!"
29 Jesus replied, "Do you believe because you see me? Happy are those
who don't see and yet believe."
30 Then Jesus did many other miraculous signs in his disciples' presence, signs that aren't recorded in this scroll. 31 But these things are
written so that you will believe that Jesus is the Christ, God's Son, and
that believing, you will have life in his name.

Jesus appears again to the disciples

21 Later, Jesus himself appeared again to his disciples at the Sea of
Tiberias. This is how it happened: 2 Simon Peter, Thomas (called

[i] Or *the twin*

Didymus[j]), Nathanael from Cana in Galilee, Zebedee's sons, and two other disciples were together. [3]Simon Peter told them, "I'm going fishing."

They said, "We'll go with you." They set out in a boat, but throughout the night they caught nothing. [4]Early in the morning, Jesus stood on the shore, but the disciples didn't realize it was Jesus.

[5]Jesus called to them, "Children, have you caught anything to eat?"

They answered him, "No."

[6]He said, "Cast your net on the right side of the boat and you will find some."

So they did, and there were so many fish that they couldn't haul in the net. [7]Then the disciple whom Jesus loved said to Peter, "It's the Lord!" When Simon Peter heard it was the Lord, he wrapped his coat around himself (for he was naked) and jumped into the water. [8]The other disciples followed in the boat, dragging the net full of fish, for they weren't far from shore, only about one hundred yards.

[9]When they landed, they saw a fire there, with fish on it, and some bread. [10]Jesus said to them, "Bring some of the fish that you've just caught." [11]Simon Peter got up and pulled the net to shore. It was full of large fish, one hundred fifty-three of them. Yet the net hadn't torn, even with so many fish. [12]Jesus said to them, "Come and have breakfast." None of the disciples could bring themselves to ask him, "Who are you?" They knew it was the Lord. [13]Jesus came, took the bread, and gave it to them. He did the same with the fish. [14]This was now the third time Jesus appeared to his disciples after he was raised from the dead.

Jesus and Peter

[15]When they finished eating, Jesus asked Simon Peter, "Simon son of John, do you love me more than these?"

Simon replied, "Yes, Lord, you know I love you."

Jesus said to him, "Feed my lambs." [16]Jesus asked a second time, "Simon son of John, do you love me?"

Simon replied, "Yes, Lord, you know I love you."

Jesus said to him, "Take care of my sheep." [17]He asked a third time, "Simon son of John, do you love me?"

Peter was sad that Jesus asked him a third time, "Do you love me?" He replied, "Lord, you know everything; you know I love you."

Jesus said to him, "Feed my sheep. [18]I assure you that when you were younger you tied your own belt and walked around wherever you wanted. When you grow old, you will stretch out your hands and

[j]Or *the twin*

another will tie your belt and lead you where you don't want to go." [19]He said this to show the kind of death by which Peter would glorify God. After saying this, Jesus said to Peter, "Follow me."

Jesus and the disciple whom he loved

[20]Peter turned around and saw the disciple whom Jesus loved following them. This was the one who had leaned against Jesus at the meal and asked him, "Lord, who is going to betray you?" [21]When Peter saw this disciple, he said to Jesus, "Lord, what about him?"

[22]Jesus replied, "If I want him to remain until I come, what difference does that make to you? You must follow me." [23]Therefore, the word spread among the brothers and sisters that this disciple wouldn't die. However, Jesus didn't say he wouldn't die, but only, "If I want him to remain until I come, what difference does that make to you?" [24]This is the disciple who testifies concerning these things and who wrote them down. We know that his testimony is true. [25]Jesus did many other things as well. If all of them were recorded, I imagine the world itself wouldn't have enough room for the scrolls that would be written.

NOTES

Chapter One

1. Russell D. Moore, "A Purpose-Driven Cosmos: Why Jesus Doesn't Promise Us an 'Afterlife,' *Christianity Today* 56 (February 2012): 33.

Chapter Two

1. "I Come with Joy," *The United Methodist Hymnal* (Nashville: The United Methodist Publishing House, 1989), 617.
2. William Barclay, *The Gospel of John*, vol. 2, The Daily Study Bible Series (Louisville: Westminster John Knox, 1975), 40.
3. "Amazing Grace," *The United Methodist Hymnal* (Nashville: The United Methodist Publishing House, 1989), 378.

Chapter Three

1. It should be noted that there is some debate among scholars concerning the precise meaning of the Hebrew word behind this name, but it seems clearly to be related to the verb to be.
2. Paul Tillich, *Systematic Theology* (Chicago: University of Chicago Press, 1951), vol. 1: 112, 116.

3. C.K. Barrett, *Essays on John* (Philadelphia: Westminster Press, 1982), 86.
4. Ignatius died in A.D. 107 (or possibly 117; there is some debate about the date of his death). There are a number of epistles that bear his name, though seven have been thought by many scholars to be genuine, including an Epistle to the Ephesians. I've drawn this quotation of Ephesians 20:2 from a translation by John Lightfoot: *A Commentary of the New Testament from the Talmud and Hebraica*. Whether Ignatius wrote these words or not, they reflect a very early way of describing the significance of Communion, likely drawn from John 6.
5. "Blest Be the Tie That Binds," *The United Methodist Hymnal* (Nashville: The United Methodist Publishing House, 1989), 557.

Chapter Four

1. Luis Andres Henao, "Argentines Celebrate Francis as Their 'Slum Pope,'" *Associated Press*, March 15, 2013, accessed September 1, 2015, http://news.yahoo.com/argentines-celebrate-francis-slum-pope-064548438.html.
2. Part of a longer prayer, this prayer is attributed to St. Patrick. St. Patrick is said to have written this prayer as he prepared to evangelize the high king of Ireland. This version is available at http://www.beliefnet.com/Prayers/Catholic/Morning/The-Prayer-Of-St-Patrick.aspx.
3. Cara Buckley, "Man Is Rescued by Stranger on Subway Tracks," *New York Times*, January 3, 2007, accessed September 1, 2015, http://www.nytimes.com/2007/01/03/nyregion/03life.html?ex=1325480400&en=bfb239e4fab06ab5&ei=5090&partner=rssuserland&_r=0/.

Chapter Five

1. Only Mark mentions that Jesus was crucified at nine in the morning, but Matthew and Luke agree it was in the morning and all three agree that it was the first day of the Feast of the Passover, not the Day of Preparation as John records.
2. For more on the story of the Afghan police officer, see http://www.huffingtonpost.com/2013/03/12/afghan-police-officer-hugs-suicide-bomber_n_2863081.html, accessed September 10, 2015.

3. For more on the story of the pediatric surgeon, see http://abcnews.go.com/beta/US/chicago-pediatric-surgeon-dies-lake-michigan-resue-attempt/story?id=16940866, accessed September 10, 2015.
4. William H. Willimon, *Thank God It's Friday* (Nashville: Abingdon Press, 2006), 62.

Chapter Six

1. "Hymn of Promise," *The United Methodist Hymnal* (Nashville: The United Methodist Publishing House, 1989), 707.
2. "When We All Get to Heaven," *The United Methodist Hymnal* (Nashville: The United Methodist Publishing House, 1989), 701.

For Further Reading

Brown, Raymond E. *The Gospel and Epistles of John: A Concise Commentary.* Collegeville, MN: Liturgical Press, 1988.

———. *The Anchor Yale Bible Commentaries.* Vol. 29 and 29A, *The Gospel According to John I-XII* and *The Gospel According to John XIII-XXI.* New Haven, CT: Yale University Press, 1995.

Keck, Leander E. *The New Interpreter's Bible Commentary.* Vol. 8, *Luke and John.* Nashville: Abingdon Press, 2015.

Kysar, Robert D. *A Short-Term Disciple Bible Study.* Vol. 5, *Invitation to John.* Nashville: Abingdon Press, 2007. (DVD also available)

———. *John: The Maverick Gospel, Third Edition.* Louisville: Westminster John Knox Press, 2007.

Michaels, J. Ramsey. *The New International Commentary on the New Testament: The Gospel of John.* Grand Rapids, MI: Eerdmans, 2010.

Newbigin, Lesslie. *The Light Has Come: An Exposition of the Fourth Gospel.* Grand Rapids, MI: Eerdmans, 1987.

O'Day, Gail R. and Susan E. Hylen. *Westminster Bible Companion. Vol. 30, John*. Louisville: Westminster John Knox Press, 2006.

Smith, D. Moody. *New Testament Theology*. Vol. 7, *The Theology of the Gospel of John*. Cambridge: Cambridge University Press, 2010.

———. *Abingdon New Testament Commentaries. John*. Nashville: Abingdon Press, 1999

Sloyan, Gerard. *Interpretation: A Bible Commentary for Teaching and Preaching*. Vol. 12, *John*. Louisville: Westminster John Knox Press, 1988.

Thompson, Marianne Meye. *The New Testament Library*. Vol. 21, *John: A Commentary*. Louisville: Westminster John Knox Press, 2015.

ACKNOWLEDGMENTS

I'm grateful for Professor Jouette Bassler, who in her first year on the faculty at Perkins School of Theology taught the course I took in Greek exegesis of John. I recall some juvenile stunts that a friend and I pulled in her class, but despite those, I absorbed what she taught and savored the texts she assigned. Her instruction in that class continues to shape my teaching and preaching on John's Gospel. My apologies to her for any shortcomings in this book and for anything in it with which she might disagree. But to the degree that the book illuminates John and his portrayal of Jesus, she deserves much of the credit.

I'm grateful to Susan Salley at Abingdon Press for her partnership in my work on most of my books during the last seven years. Likewise, Ron Kidd's editorial work makes each of these books eminently more readable. Thank you, Ron, for your suggestions to improve the text. Thanks also to Jill Reddig, who helped organize the inital draft of this book, and to the entire Abingdon team.

Thank you to Harry Leake, Chuck Long, and the video team at United Methodist Communications for their excellent work in producing the small group videos that accompany this study. I'm also grateful to the young pastors and staff members who joined as the "studio audience" for the videos.

This book, like many of my books, began as a sermon series that I shared with The Church of the Resurrection several years ago. I love this congregation and am grateful for their willingness to allow me to write.

Finally, I want to thank my wife, LaVon Hamilton, who tolerates my late nights and the many times I write during my day off or on vacation in order to prepare this and the other books I've written. She is my partner in ministry and in faith, and I am profoundly grateful for her.

Made in the USA
Columbia, SC
13 March 2023